it's not
necessarily
not the
truth

it's not
necessarily
not the truth

dreaming bigger
than the town
you're from

JAIME PRESSLY

WILLIAM MORROW

An Imprint of HarperCollins*Publishers*

I have changed the names of some individuals, and modified identifying features, including physical descriptions and occupations, of other individuals in order to preserve their anonymity. In some cases, composite characters have been created or timelines have been compressed, in order to further preserve privacy and to maintain narrative flow. The goal in all cases was to protect people's privacy without damaging the integrity of the story.

FIRST EDITION

Designed by Chris Welch

Library of Congress Cataloging-in-Publication Data has been applied for.

ISBN 978-0-06-145414-1

09 10 11 12 13   OV/RRD   10 9 8 7 6 5 4 3 2 1

For Dezi James
My son, my inspiration, my love

CONTENTS

it's not

necessarily

not the

truth

story

In the beginning was the word.

Where I'm from, the knowledge and acceptance of that basic fact is a given. So much so I think it could be considered an unofficial slogan for the South. Not only because of religion and the role it plays in places like North Carolina, where I was born and raised—that would be way too obvious and literal, especially for a group of folk who subsist on subtext. In the South, when people talk about the power of the word, they could be making reference to God and any of the gospels in the Bible. But then again, they could be alluding to folklore, pure and simple, or any other type of tale with a sage message hidden deep inside of it. After all, we're a people who believe in the sort of salvation that comes from a well-told story. And it doesn't matter who's doing the telling—could be a deacon or the Devil himself—just as long as he does it right.

Storytelling is as common a pastime in the South as eating a plate of collard greens or fried green tomatoes. That's probably because people from the South lead such complicated lives, and talking is another form of untangling, figuring out how, where, and why things fit together. Or maybe it's because we just like living out loud, taking our everyday experiences and turning them into a song, or a prayer, or an anecdote to be shared during supper. I can't really speak to the reasons why, but what I do know for sure is that already, throughout history, we've sung new musical genres into creation and written volumes of prose based on nothing more than all the actions and interactions that take place underneath the gentle, unassuming façade of our run-of-the-mill, small-town lives.

It makes sense then that what I remember most about my youth is the stories I was told, stories about the people around me—friends, family members, and the array of neighbors I'd known since the day I was born. They were a proverbial motley crew, these people, a cast of the most comical, quietly controversial, and unadulterated characters anyone could ever imagine. I learned to lose myself in their stories, absorbing the complexities of their choices and the intricacies of their secrets. I would sit, drop-jawed, taking it all in until I became far too intimate with their sorrows and regrets and overly invested in their quests for happiness.

Some people look back and measure their growth in years or

with events. When they tell you about their first kiss or the first time somebody asked them to dance, they might recall that it was on a balmy November night in 1984, or that it was during the school dance which took place the first Friday after Ronald Reagan won the presidential election. More often than not, I tend to measure my growth with stories, with all the words that swirled around each significant achievement, each new awareness, as it was happening.

I remember, for instance, when and where I first gained a sense of myself as an individual, a person with wants and needs that were specifically her own. It was after I'd heard about my grandmother's penchant for bargain-hunting, especially twofers—except, in her case, "fourfers" would be the more appropriate word—four for the price of one. With four young boys and one girl at her feet, my Grandmamma Pressly, as the story was told, was a firm believer in the "one fell swoop" philosophy. She kept all of her boys in buzz cuts, because it was easier, and when one of them needed a trim, she'd gather the whole bunch and march them right down to the barbershop, even if their hair hadn't grown an inch since their last cut.

The same applied to appointments with doctors and dentists, as well as trips to the department store. When one of her boys needed to have his wisdom teeth removed, she piled the rest of them into the car too, figuring that even though they weren't having problems now, they'd eventually have to have a tooth pulled, wisdom or other, so now was as good a time as any, since she'd more than likely get a discount for bringing in that many patients.

I'll never forget how grateful I was, after hearing that story, to be the only girl and also to have a brother who was nine and a half years older than me. I'd always been somebody with a strong personality and an unflinching knowledge of her likes and dislikes as well as her needs and wants. But I'd never before appreciated that having them met was a privilege, not until I considered the existence of an alternative. I couldn't even begin to imagine being made to wear the same haircut or style as somebody else just because we were siblings, or having to go to the doctor and get poked and prodded just because somebody else was sick.

It might seem like a negligible piece of enlightenment, but when you're six or seven, as I was, it's actually a major revelation. It's like having a thin layer of film lifted off your world, a film you never even knew was there, which allows you to see things a little bit clearer. That's the effect each and every one of those stories my family members told me had; they altered my impressions of places, of people and things. They gave me insight.

As of right now, I've spent exactly as many years living away from my hometown as I did living in it. No matter how far away I've moved from my past, in miles or in memory, I've always carried those stories with me. Even though I return every year to visit, I've never, as the saying goes, been able to go home again. So much has changed. Some people have died. Others, like me, have moved far away. And those who have chosen to remain have been in constant motion—gaining weight or losing hair, giving birth or getting divorced. Nothing has stood still in time, except, of course, those stories, all those words and the voices that spoke them.

For several weeks I'd been thinking a lot about those words, those voices. I'd been going over the stories again and again, using them to map my maturity, to gauge how far I've come. I'd been surrounding myself with an assortment of voices, from my Granddaddy and Grandmamma Presslys' to my parents' and my uncles' and aunts'. It was like a chorus, a warm tapestry of sound. The voices greeted me with soft chants every morning when I awoke, their free rhythms fluttered around me like butterfly wings as I went through my day, and their melodies serenaded me as I drifted into sleep.

It all started when I found out I was pregnant. I went out and bought every book on pregnancy and childbirth on the market. It was my first time and I wanted a step-by-step manual, something to explain what I should expect, what I might experience. Page by page, I pored through those books, reading them first in their entirety and then referring back to certain sections when I reached crucial stages in every week of each trimester. And then one day I read something that pulled my past into sharp focus, made me start going over my life's stories.

What I read was that my fetus—every fetus, in fact—was able to hear, and hear quite well, from the second trimester on. The author of the book where I'd read that went on to encourage parents to speak or sing to their unborn babies. "Start reading them books, or telling them stories," she suggested. It wasn't as if I didn't already know this. I'd heard about expectant parents

placing headphones on the mother's protruding belly and playing classical music for their babies, or fathers kneeling every
night in front of their pregnant wives and speaking straight
into their navel as if it were a microphone.

I'd even already started talking to my own unborn son, telling him that I love him, giving him colorful descriptions of my
activities, and preparing him for uncomfortable situations.
"Okay, Dezi," I'd say to him before lunch. "I'm going to order
a Caesar salad and a tall glass of water for us." "Hold on, little
one," I'd warn him as I was driving. "This road is kinda bumpy."
And always, always, throughout each day, I'd let him know that
he is the best thing to ever happen in my life.

So, you see, what I read wasn't surprising in any way, shape,
or form. But it did make me think, especially the part about
telling stories. It was still early in my pregnancy. I hadn't even
officially announced it to the world. All I'd been doing in those
initial weeks was holding conversations with Dezi, telling him
about how I felt, what I was doing, giving him clues about the
here and now. But after reading what I read, I realized it was
probably time to move on to more.

So came the tough questions. What stories would I share
with Dezi? Nursery rhymes and picture books were all well and
good but if sound was going to be my baby's introduction to the
outside world, then I wanted it to be the sound of a story being
told Pressly-style, with all the inflections and dramatic pauses,
the eyebrow-lifting irony and thunderous laughter which mark
every tale we tell. I wanted to relate those stories to him in the

tradition of our family, again and again, until they seeped from my skin right into his skin, and settled into his soul.

That's when I summoned the voices, started recounting the stories—all of them. There were my all-time favorites and some that I didn't care for at all. There were the ones that I knew, beyond a shadow of a doubt, were real and true, and some that I wasn't so sure about—the ones that were not necessarily flat-out fibs but not necessarily not the truth. I started collecting them, carefully organizing them the way people organize photographs in an album, for posterity.

I never used to think of myself as much of a storyteller. Not an original one, anyway. For a long time, when it came to stories, I was more of a repeater than a teller. I suppose that was as it should have been, because I was young. There was nothing to look back on. All the elements and events were just coming together. Whatever stories I could one day tell, stories that were distinctly my own, were still being shaped, but that didn't stop me from telling other people's stories every chance I got, repeating them like they were mine.

If imitation is the highest form of flattery, then my family knows how much I love them, 'cause by the time I was old enough to ride my bike, I had each one of them down pat. I knew how to hold court like my Granddaddy Pressly, to sit in the center of a circle with all eyes and ears focused on me to get the story started right. I also knew how to crescendo like Uncle Pruitt did as the plot was reaching its climactic parts; how to use my hands for added expression like my Uncle Ezra did; or use my eyes to speak for me whenever I grew silent, like my Aunt Careen did. Each of them contributed something to what soon became my repertoire of storytelling skills. However, the one lesson I didn't learn until much later is that stories, like scars, are earned. They're reminders not so much of the storms we've weathered but of the wonder that we survived.

It takes a whole heck of a lot of courage to speak your own story, to stand there naked in front of everybody, displaying your scars. I didn't realize that until the first time I tried and came up silent. The pain was still too raw for me to turn it into laughter, and everybody knows a good story has to have at least a smidgen of humor in it, even if it's only to help tease along the tears.

So I started to write it all down. Not for the sake of the story but for the sake of the healing. Each of those early words was a balm. I would lay them down, ink on paper, for their ability to soothe. Later, I would fold those sheets of paper, my little testimonies, into halves, and then quarters, and I would hide them in a secret mementos box for safekeeping, for the time being.

It'd been years since I'd touched that box or thought about those stories I'd written down, all of them still in the beginning stages, not fully developed. For weeks, my family's voices had kept me company. I'd grown used to the companionship, used to hearing them in my head recounting the stories I'd heard throughout my youth. But one day they just stopped as suddenly as they had started.

I was sitting in my rocking chair, holding a copy of *Goodnight Moon* in my hand. I'd just finished reading it aloud. It made me all nostalgic, got me thinking about the Carolina sky, and that, of course, made me think of my Granddaddy Pressly. And that, of course, made me want to share one of his stories with Dezi, who was wide-awake, practicing karate kicks in my womb.

I closed my eyes and tried to summon my granddaddy's voice, so that I could listen to him telling the story, but I couldn't hear a thing. I tried summoning another voice, my Grandmamma Pressly's. Now, she was somebody who always had something to say. Still nothing, not a single word. The only thing that came to me was an image of that dusty ole box in the back of my closet. I was getting worried, wondering why I couldn't hear them anymore, then the craziest thought started running through my head: what if I shared one of my own stories with Dezi instead?

I considered getting up to go get the box but I was comfortable in that chair. Pregnancy can wear a woman out, make her stay put in one place. Anyway, there was really no point in expending that energy because I knew every word on those sheets by heart. And to prove it to myself, I started reciting one of the stories in my head, confidently, effortlessly. It felt so natural to me that I didn't even bother to spend a moment or a breath worrying about the fact that none of those stories in that box had endings. I had left them all unfinished. For some reason that didn't matter. I felt sure that if I kept going like I was, the story would find its own path, know when to bend, when to break, and when to come to a complete stop.

So I opened my mouth, suddenly very sure of myself, and started to speak. "Settle down now, Dezi," I said. "Mama's gonna tell you a story."

celebrity

Surely you've heard of the Hatfields and the McCoys. They're two families of hard-drinking, gun-toting hillbillies from Appalachia, who tried, generation after generation, to kill each other off—first, over a pig, and then, later, over things that were a little bit more sensible than swine, things like lust and love and loss—three undeniable staples of the South. Not that their reasons for fighting ended up mattering much in the end. Truth be told, reasons always seem to somehow get lost in the shuffle of rage and the judgments of memory. It was the actual feud that made them famous, the Hatfields and the McCoys. Nothing more than that long, bitter feud, which, at this point, has become generic, a symbol sucked dry of all its meaning.

I guess you could say that, in a way, I got my first taste of fame from that same kind of fighting, the kind that splits up kinfolk and makes blood turn as bad as fruit left hanging on the vine. Except, in this case, the feud only involved one family—mine.

I was born in 1977, just two and a half weeks shy of the day that Elvis Presley up and died in Graceland. My hometown, Kinston, was about as close to Memphis as the moon is to Greenville, which was the closest thing to a real city that we North Carolina kids living by the coast knew. With a population of twenty-three thousand, on a section of land a little less than seventeen square miles, Kinston was barely big enough to be considered a town, let alone a city.

Even so, everybody there had heard of the King. Heck, they even talked about him like he lived just down the block and was liable to show up at any minute inside the Dairy Bar over on East Bern Road to order up one of their legendary cheeseburgers with a large root-beer float. There were plenty of Elvis sightings alright. Left to that grapevine gab alone, he was likely to saunter into any establishment in Lenoir County that had a jukebox, Formica tables, and a well-stocked tray of condiments. Even though so many years had passed since he'd hit his last note, people seemed more eager to place their faith in the far-fetched than to actually face the fact that Elvis Presley was dead. He was really and truly gone.

By the time I started school, all it took was a mention of my name for the whole kindergarten class to break out in an impromptu, off-key version of "Blue Suede Shoes" or "Jailhouse Rock." That's because my family's last name is Pressly. The

spellings are different, but the two names, Pressly and Presley, are pronounced the same. But kindergartners don't give
a cracked Crayola about the distinctions of spelling, so I got
slammed with all kinda cockamamie questions: "Are you related to Elvis?" "Is it true that he's still alive?" "Tell me, what's
Lisa Marie like?" When I came up blank on answers, I got ridi-
culed and beat down by the rows of long lashes that shaded
those kids' skeptical glares. So I gathered up all of those questions and carried them to the single person I knew for sure
could teach me the truth: my Granddaddy Pressly.

"Of course Elvis Aron is our kin," said Granddaddy Pressly.
"And don't let nobody tell you any different." We were in his and
Grandmamma Pressly's yard, sitting inside the white gazebo.
His legs looked so long; long and bent, spiderlike, and he held
my hand as he wove those convoluted webs. Call it revisionist
history.

"Chicken," he continued. In those days, pet names were literal: monkey, chipmunk, possum, bunny, bird. "Chicken" was
the one my daddy had chosen for me, because he was something
of a mama's boy and it was the nickname Granddaddy Pressly
used to call Grandmamma Pressly. "Years and years ago,"
Granddaddy explained, "long before any of us ever had the notion to learn to forgive and let bygones be bygones, there was a
big ole fight that just tore our family apart, ripped it damn near
to shreds. Figurin' the fat lady done sang and it was all over but
the shoutin', half of 'em—the Presleys—picked up, went to Tennessee, and never came back. The other half, our branch of the
brood, stayed their ground. But we made our own move toward

creatin' distance with the past by changin' the family name, addin' an extra s and droppin' that last e. That's how we became known as Pressly instead of Presley."

Granddaddy patted me on the back. Discussion done, he stood up, stretched a spell, then slid each index finger into a belt loop and pulled up his trousers. He always wore his pants up really high, like he knew that one day the small puddle in the basement was gonna spread out and eventually rise up onto the first floor, and he wanted to be right and ready for it.

I've never been a quick believer, but I had to stop and ask myself, *What if? What if Elvis Presley was really and truly my distant cousin?*

"You sure that's the truth, Granddaddy?" I asked, tugging on one of those loops he'd just let go of. He told me to think about it, to weigh everything he'd said and everything I already knew real carefully, and then to judge for myself.

"Chicken, you can always see the truth if you look close enough."

Right as Granddaddy Pressly may have been, the beauty of the South is that folks are darned good about fixing up things and doing whatever it takes to make 'em look like the truth. It gets so you can't hardly see to tell the difference between what's real and what's being projected. And it ain't always because you're slow, or gullible, or plain stupid, with a capital S. We've all, even the best of us, taken plenty of turns at playing that kind of fool. That's just the way of the culture, at least it was where I grew up.

The Kinston, North Carolina, of my youth was a really quaint place with beautiful homes, lots of red brick and shutters, and streets as wide and smoothly bent as old rivers. Everything was well manicured. The grass was cut low, the hedges were always trimmed. There were lots and lots of trees—dogwoods and pines and weeping willows—lining the driveways. Gardens boasted roses in bushes and shrubs all around—polyanthus, blessings, and solitaires. Every few houses, you could even see climbing American beauties, their blooms threatening to reach the top of the porch railings for a peek.

People prided themselves on taking care of their lawns and going to church. But being that we were in extremely close proximity to the so-called Buckle of the Bible Belt, nobody waited until Sunday to wear their finest, or to speak the Lord's name, be it in praise or in vain. Since everybody knew everybody else, fellowship was about as regular as any other daily activity, stirring up as much evil as it did good. You had to have a dictionary to translate all the double-talk that went on in that town. Usually, when somebody came up, smiled, and said, "Well, ain't you just looking special today?" what they really meant was, *Loooord, who let this child out the house wearing* that? And it'd be a downright miracle if that person didn't say it out loud to the individual sitting next to them the minute you turned around and walked out of earshot.

You weren't supposed to go out without wearing clean clothes and having your hair "did." And nobody gave a hoot if your whole life was falling apart behind the scenes, being held together by paper clips and Prozac, you were expected to somehow pull it together whenever you stepped foot out your front door.

Though it was kinda petty and disingenuous, decorum like that built a whole lot of good fences, because it made for polite neighbors and a peaceful, aesthetic environment. I guess the abiding belief was that setting a certain standard would bring everybody to the same level. It would turn "ordinary" into something acceptable, something everyone could achieve or, at the very least, strive to achieve. The few people who were somehow able to break free of those mores to create their own code of conduct were held at arm's length and regarded with suspicion, because, well, they were certifiably crazy. Once in a while, within a certain context, they were referred to as courageous— a word which you eventually come to understand is nothing more, in that climate, than a mere synonym for "crazy."

Given all this, I could see—with extreme clarity, I must say—that everything Granddaddy Pressly told me was not only possible, it was absolutely probable. First off were the family features. All of us, Pressly and Presley, had that same easy smile, which might as well have been trademarked. It was as contagious as it was crooked. Then there were those high, chiseled cheeks, and that stare, clear and bright and undeniable, nearly primal in its attraction. I had to concede, though, that the teeth, all straight and square and paper-white like Chiclets, could very well be a coincidence, since oral hygiene is, and has always been, an important part of proper Southern breeding. Lots of people living below the Mason-Dixon Line have good teeth—unless, of course, they chew tobacco or use snuff.

More telling than any of that flesh-and-bone stuff, though, was the sameness of our spirit. Like the King, the Presslys weren't nothing if we weren't for show. We were, each and every one of us, filled with the sort of life that could only be lived fully on a stage, in front of an appreciative audience. You didn't have to go very far back into our family tree to prove that. Granddaddy owned and ran Pressly's Laundry, and Grandmamma was a beautician; she even started the cosmetology school at the local college. And you'd better believe that they sure enough didn't spend all that time helping others bring out their star-quality to not place a hefty investment on fostering it in their own kids.

They had five children, not counting the very first one, Linda, who died before she was even a year old. Everybody in Kinston knew the Presslys. There's Careen, who is five-eleven, tall, graceful, and exotic. With a bottle of Coppertone and an afternoon of sunshine on her skin, she'd be a dead ringer for Tina Turner. And then there're "the boys": Pruitt, Zane, Ezra, and J. L., my dad. They were known as the best dancers in town. They knew how to "shag" and "twist," do "the locomotion" and "the mashed potato."

Whenever there was an event in town and one of them hit the floor, word would spread through the room like a ripple on the surface of water. All the women wanted to dance with them. And don't let there be more than one of them out there. "The Presslys are on the floor," folks would call out, as they moved in closer to the action. "The Presslys are on the floor." A crowd would gather. Everybody would stop what they were doing and start elbowing their way to the front, so they could watch the Pressly boys cut a rug.

Ah, the "Pressly boys"; their glory days were the stuff of legend—all of them, especially my dad, who was about as cool as a tall glass of mint julep in the suffocating heat of mid-July. That man has always had the gift of style and charisma. They even made him head of the Prep Club at his school. Whether he was wearing his military school uniform, starched and pressed stiff with razor-sharp creases, or one of his many soft cardigan sweaters, J. L. Pressly was usually dressed so slick he could have easily been mistaken for one of those male models in the department-store catalogs—like J. Crew or L. L. Bean or The Gap or Sears. Well, maybe not Sears, but you get the general idea.

Whenever Dad or any of the other "Pressly boys" would tell me stories about back then, in their heyday, I was somehow able to channel all that energy from those memories straight into my body, into every muscle, every organ, ligament, and sinew. The feeling was almost palpable, like a living, breathing thing, and I knew I was tapping into that certain something that made them so special, so magnetic. People were drawn to them because of it, that spark, that thingamajiggy, a *je ne sais quoi* that nobody can put their finger on, but everybody knows is one of the key ingredients in the recipe for celebrity. The "Pressly boys" were destined for fame and fortune. It was in the stars. And I used to sincerely believe they would have realized that destiny—had they left Kinston and set their sights on a larger stage.

I've heard people say that Kinston is "God's country," heard them say you couldn't find a more beautiful stretch of earth

unless it was in a place called Paradise. It is definitely picturesque, the perfect setting for a Sunday afternoon drive. But,
growing up, the thing I loved the most about Kinston was far
above the ground: I loved the sky, the famous Carolina sky, that
huge, bright sweep of blue that hung over us, all peaceful and
still, like a preview of heaven. On the not-so-sunshiny days,
the patterns and cycles of the clouds were an endless source
of fascination to me. The rest of the town seemed unchang-
ing, permanently set in a particular way. What I loved about
the sky was its unpredictability. You never really knew what to
expect. One night it could be studded with silver, stars twinkling, twinkling, twinkling every which way you looked. The
next night, it could be as blank and empty of inspiration as a
substitute teacher's blackboard.

I spent hours upon hours staring up at that sky, watching or
waiting, wondering and wishing. It expanded the limits of the
town for me. It convinced me that the possibilities this world
held for me were infinite, and I sure as heck needed them to
be, because by the time I hit puberty, I already knew that my
dreams were far too big for a town as small as Kinston. Especially since my dreams weren't just my own. They were an
amalgamation, the dreams of my parents and of my grandparents, and the dreams of my uncles and aunt as well.

Now, this doesn't mean that the members of my family didn't
have the gumption or wherewithal to see to their own dreams.
They did, and, to the best of my knowledge, most of the dreams
they had for themselves came true. But along the way, some of
those dreams, as is always the case in life, fell by the wayside.

Even worse, some of them were written off as fantasies, unrealistic imaginings that are only tolerated when they come from the idle, the rich, or from society's excusably immature and irrational—the children. Those were the dreams, those stale little breadcrumbs left in the forest, that I picked up and decided to keep for myself.

I dreamed of dancing on a stage, singing into a microphone, acting in front of a camera, seeing a full-size picture of myself on the glossy page of a magazine. What I really wanted, however it came to me, was to own that feeling I'd experienced through the stories of the "Pressly boys." I wanted to get it all firsthand, that rush and that pride. I wanted to stand tall in honor of myself the same way that, after talking to Granddaddy Pressly that day, I'd started to stand tall in honor of my long-lost cousin, the late great Elvis Presley.

I know, I know; every young girl in America with a cute smile and a smidgen of talent dreams of celebrity. Still, I felt that my situation was different, that I was different. I'd been taking lessons for so long I couldn't tell you which I started doing first, dancing or walking. I sang scales, sang old Motown hits, lullabies, Christmas carols; I even sang top-forty songs in the shower. The hard work didn't scare me, and the discipline was almost second nature. But those things alone weren't extraordinary, not in the performing arts. What made me feel set apart from every other Jane, Sue, and Kathy wannabe was this sense of inevitability.

Of course I was gonna make it; I had to. It was a part of me. After all, it ran in the family; it was in my blood.

I'm not sure exactly how, when, or why it started to dawn on me that Granddaddy Pressly had probably told me a fib, that this feud he'd went on and on about, the unresolved fight that sent one group of our kinfolk running across state lines and the other changing the spelling of the family name, probably never happened. Elvis Presley was probably no more my distant cousin than Jamie Lee Curtis is my fraternal twin.

Maybe I'd suspected it all along, right from the get-go, in the same way a whole lot of kids suspect that there isn't some big, fat, bearded man in a red suit sliding down people's chimneys on Christmas Eve, or some magical winged creature going from bedroom to bedroom taking recently lost teeth that have been left underneath pillows and replacing them with cash. Their existence defies logic and good common sense—but don't think for a minute kids don't know this. Yet and still, seeing as how kids spend more time looking and listening than anything else, on account of the fact that adults rarely ever let them talk too much or touch too many things, they also know that seeing something doesn't make it real, and *not* seeing something doesn't make it *un*real.

See, the difference between kids and adults is that even in the face of certain doubt, kids still ask themselves, *What if?* They still hold out hope and give the world a chance to provide an answer. I guess that's why my Granddaddy Pressly told me that story. It wasn't about passing off a lie as the truth. Granddaddy Pressly knew I was at my wits' end, on the verge of letting those kids at school write me off as a "nobody" 'cause I couldn't speak up and claim that I was somebody. Somebody important.

I think what Granddaddy Pressly wanted was to have me take a closer look at our community and our family—to see who we really were, and to know what I was really made of. He wanted me to ask *What if?* and to keep on asking that for as long as it took. My granddaddy knew that one day, as I got closer to being grown, something or somebody was gonna convince me to stop asking, but he also knew that it wouldn't matter, because by then, I would already have discovered all the answers I needed to fully become the person I was meant to be.

redemption

For such a small place, my hometown, Kinston, has surely ushered some pretty big names out into the world. The famous jazz and funk musician Maceo Parker—as well as his brothers, Melvin and Kellis, famous in their own right—were born and raised there. Maceo, who's probably the best-known of the three, has played with everybody from James Brown, Ray Charles, and George Clinton, to James Taylor, Ani DiFranco, and the Red Hot Chili Peppers.

Jerry Stackhouse, the NBA star, is also a native son. I went to high school with him, was a cheerleader during the time that he was the number one basketball player. Not just number one in the school or the town, either, but number one in the entire state. He went on to play for the University of North Carolina, and when he was a sophomore, Jerry was named College Player of the Year by *Sports Illustrated* and featured on the cover of the magazine. Talk about phenomenal!

Jerry Stackhouse and those Parker brothers, they made our town proud. Back when I was still in school there, everybody loved them so much they probably would've given their eye-teeth to have any one of those men sit at their table for supper, because they were our heroes. And they were talented, success-ful, extraordinarily so. I can't say I'm as sure if the same level of open-door hospitality would be so readily extended to the average African-American Joe in town. That might have been a little too close for the comfort of the good white folks of Kinston—who were, incidentally and ironically, fast becoming the minority population there. I suppose a lot of towns in the South are still like that; the citizens—black, white, gay, straight—live side by side, peacefully if not equally. They might mix and mingle, but probably only on the most superficial of levels, like at sporting events and other common-interest gatherings in public spaces. And while that may be all well and good, when it comes to personal matters or private events, they're about as far apart as Albania and Zimbabwe, and never the twain shall meet.

The South has, traditionally, been a bastion of prejudice and separatism, what with groups and individuals like the White Patriot Party, the Ku Klux Klan, Strom Thurmond, and David Duke. Obviously, I'm generalizing. There are lots of people from the South who are open-minded and fair, and believe in the guarantees of freedom and the pursuit of happiness for everyone, as stipulated in the Constitution of these United States. There were many times, however, when I still lived in the South, that I felt like its infamous legacy of hatred and oppression was aggressively pervasive. It seemed to be in the air that we breathed, and the water that we drank. It was like a poison, seeping into the healthiest hearts and the most reasonable minds, corrupting people who were otherwise fair and decent and upright, people like my very own father.

Tyrone Lamont Johnson was a boy in my kindergarten class who had a crush on me. The affection was mutual; I had a crush on him, too. Then again, by the age of five, I was already boy-crazy. I had a crush on pretty much everybody in the classroom at the time. One day, Tyrone sent me a note. It was on one of those huge, light-beige-colored, extra-wide-ruled sheets of paper that teachers reserve for kids who're just learning how to write. Using gigantic letters, half of which were leaning in one direction, looking like they were about to fall off the edge of the paper, Tyrone had written: *Will you go with me? Check the box yes or no.* He'd drawn two empty boxes, ballot-style, with *yes* written beside one and *no* written beside the other. It was the most adorable little gesture you could imagine, though it wasn't especially original; that's how all the elementary-school boys, from kindergarten to third grade, found their girlfriends. The older kids didn't send notes. They actually asked in person or on the phone.

I put the note in my backpack so I could look at it again and again when I got home. After school, as was my routine, I went outside to play in the neighborhood. My two cousins, Madison and Gayle, who were the daughters of my uncle Pruitt, lived around one corner, and my best friend, Ruthie Hathaway, lived right around another corner. The afternoons would usually find me trying to distribute the pleasure of my company equally among the three of them until I either got too tired from running around or too ornery from hunger, and decided to go in for supper.

On this particular day, while I was gone, my dad went into my backpack, in search of a pencil or pen, I imagine. What he found was that note from Tyrone, neatly folded and tucked into a sliver of a pocket in the front compartment of the backpack, a space that seemed to be intended for money or tickets or other little slips of paper. Dad read the note and apparently hit the roof right away. He took the note, and his rage, straight to Mom, who tried her best to calm him down.

"Who cares, J. L.?" she asked him. "He's a sweet little boy. Besides, I know his mama."

"What!?!" Dad exploded. "I care, Andrea. I care, that's who!!!!" That's the point at which I walked in, while my father was yelling and fussing like somebody had done him a serious wrong, something worth stepping outside and rolling up sleeves over.

"What's going on?" I wanted to know. We aren't an especially mild-mannered family. You could say that our cup runneth over with personality and idiosyncrasy, definitely a lively bunch of folk. Still, it was clear that Dad wasn't being loud for the sake of it. He was having a conniption. "What's wrong?" I asked, not really scared, but concerned. Dad showed me the note, which he was holding in his hand, waving around like a flag in front of a bull. It took me a while to realize what it was, but when I finally did, I was completely crushed to find out that my father had invaded my privacy and gone through my things.

"You are not," he warned me, his voice stern as a principal's, "to get letters like this again from any little boys. Understand?"

For years, I thought my dad had gotten so upset because the note was a sign that his little girl was growing up. What never occurred to me was the possibility that he might have taken one look at the name on the note—Tyrone, which was not the sort of name generally given to the white children in our community— and figured that he needed, right then and there, to school me on some harsh realities of life. In an effort—misguided as it may have been—to protect his little girl, my father probably decided to let me know that getting personally involved, at any age, with a black male, would leave me open to criticism and condemnation, to the sort of vicious rumors and behind-your-back whispers that irreparably destroyed the reputations of young girls. Little did any of us know that I would spend my entire life saying, doing, and believing in things that would inspire such rumors, that I would be the sort of girl who dated whomever she liked, without any regard for what the local bigots might think or say about it.

My father wasn't a bigot, but he'd been brought up to hold people who were different at a distance. It was a situation of "them" and "us," though not necessarily "them *versus* us." Yet whenever there's a line separating individuals, stereotypes are

formed, judgments are made, and rules are set in place to protect people from that which they know very little about but fear
anyway. Dad had never really had a reason to think through, let
alone challenge, any of the preconceived notions that he'd so
blindly accepted simply because they were a part of the status
quo. Not until his brother Ezra, who'd been living in San Francisco, came back to Kinston and came out as a homosexual.

Uncle Ezra, whose actual name was Jonathan Ezra, was the
youngest of my dad's four siblings. He was tall, with dark, dark
hair, the kind that is so soft and shiny you have to stop yourself
from reaching out and running your fingers through it. He'd
been married for three years, but things fell apart with his wife
and they split up. After the divorce, Uncle Ezra traveled out to
California and stayed there for a year or two. When he moved
back, it was with a significant other, a man. Knowing that this
information would be hard for his brother to swallow, Uncle
Ezra asked my mom, who wasn't just a mere in-law but also a
close friend, to tell my dad.

"He'll take it better coming from you, Andie," Uncle Ezra assured my mother. So she agreed to be the messenger, a job that
everybody knows can oftentimes be deadly. If J. L. Pressly was
adamantly opposed to his daughter having an innocent kindergarten courtship with a black boy, then there are no words
to describe how he felt about having a gay brother. When my
mother broke the news, he was at a total loss for words. Back
then, he was working with his father over at Pressly's Laundry. It'd been a long day and what Mom said threw him completely off-kilter. He couldn't make heads or tails of it. His little

brother was what? *Gay?!!!??* How could that be? He took it as a personal affront.

Infuriated, Dad decided to go straight to the source and find out for himself. He grabbed his keys and jacket, got into his car, and screeched away. Mom tried to stop him but he bolted out of there so fast, she barely had time to get her slippers on. Dad was seeing red. When he arrived at Uncle Ezra's, he skipped right over the questions and proceeded to beat the crap out of his brother, thinking maybe he could whip the gay out of him, exorcise the homosexual demons that had possessed his otherwise normal, heterosexual body. Dad hit Uncle Ezra a few times, but then he stopped and came to his senses long before any real damage was done. He realized what he was doing, beating his own brother up like a common stranger, and it sickened him more than anything Uncle Ezra had, or could have, done. But all that anger was still in him, curled up like a comma, a brief pause before the next statement it was about to make. Confused, Dad just turned around and left, carrying his shame into the night.

There's not much you can say to defend behavior like that, but it was fear that drove my dad to do what he did. Fear and ignorance. He was afraid *for* his brother, afraid of what stepping across that boundary, leaving the familiarity and safety of "us" and stepping into the foreign territory of "them" might mean for him, for the entire family. Nobody knew better than my dad how closed a community Kinston was, how the choices an individual made in a place like that followed them, defined them, for the rest of their natural lives.

_____

Our family, like most in the area, is a mix of every group of people whose feet—collectively speaking—have ever touched Kinston soil. There has always been a significant population of Native Americans in North Carolina, the most prominent tribes being the Cherokee, Algonquian, Hatteras, and Tuscarora. The French were the first of the many European settlers in the North Carolina area. They arrived a whole two centuries before North Carolina officially became an English colony. Since most Southerners, no matter their color or creed, don't want to shake that family tree too violently or controversially, they just claim the ancestry that's closest to their likeness—no pun intended. Granddaddy Pressly's folk were mostly Scottish. Grandmamma Pressly's family, the Rochelles, were through-and-through French, even though she didn't speak or understand word one of the language.

Grandmamma Pressly, née Mary Anna Rochelle, was the seventh of eight children born to Isaac (Ike) Sloan Rochelle and Eleanor (Lena) Olivia Rochelle, née Rhodes. Ike Rochelle, my great-granddaddy, who died a good decade and a half before I was born, was a man of tremendous means. By trade, he was a farmer, a carpenter and contractor, just a regular, down-to-earth kind of guy who enjoyed working with his hands. A lot of the homes in Kinston were built by him. He owned acres and acres of land and maintained a few sideline businesses, too, like a sawmill facility and a veterinary medicine practice. Grangier High School is located on the old Rochelle sawmill site. The family also gave another plot of their land to the city so that a public middle school could be built on it. That school, which was aptly named Rochelle Middle School, is where I attended the sixth through the eighth grades.

Over the years, Kinston has gone through some tremendous changes in its landscape and its residents. During Ike Rochelle's era, there were lots and lots of farms and wide-open spaces. The Native Americans, who were still being called Indians, lived mostly on reservations throughout the state; and the blacks, who were barely out of slavery, were mainly share-croppers and domestics.

It's hard for me to imagine a time like that, a time when a person's skin color could automatically dictate his or her station in life. But that's how it was in my grandmamma's day. She came from a culture and a way of life in which people worked for her; they called her "ma'am" and avoided making direct eye contact when she talked to them. Usually, those people were black. "Colored people" is what she called them, those who worked for her. In Grandmamma's mind, "colored" must have been a term of endearment, because she used a completely different word for the black people who were strangers, the ones she didn't know and didn't care a lick about.

Grandmamma Pressly looked and smelled like privilege. She was radiant, with wide eyes, full lips, high cheekbones, and a big ole bubble butt that was handed down rather generously to her daughter and granddaughters. She didn't believe in women dressing like men; you wouldn't catch her dead in a pair of pants. She was always in a dress, with bright pink lipstick and her hair expertly coiffed, right down to the last misbehaving cowlick.

She lived in the biggest house on her block, a gorgeous white two-story Victorian with tall, white columns. It was surrounded by plenty of land, more than enough to build another house on and still have a sizable garden left over. There were lots of beautiful fig trees around the sides of the property. We had all of our holiday meals and family reunions there. One of my favorite places at Granddaddy and Grandmamma Presslys' was the big white gazebo in their yard. Sometimes I'd go in there to sit and think, but mostly it's where I would listen to people tell stories about our family—Granddaddy Pressly, Aunt Careen, my dad, even my uncle Ezra. Especially my uncle Ezra. They'd sit and spin yarns, yards and yards of them, tell me stories about what Kinston was like before I was born, what they were like.

When my dad was a senior in high school, he dated a girl named Verna Nell Cox. She was a Native American, had dark raven hair, shiny as a doll's, which she wore in a bob. She was about three years younger than him, but they had been dating for a good long while. Then, out of nowhere, my dad ended things. It just about broke Verna Nell's heart, because she was so in love with him. But Dad saw an opening, so he took the chance. He got lucky, and started dating another girl, Lacy Waller, somebody he'd always been sweet on. She was also Native American and looked an awful lot like her rival, Verna Nell, except Lacy was a little older. She was also extremely popular in school, the "it" girl. She and my dad fell madly in love with each other. In his mind, this was the girl for him, "the one."

Dad and Lacy had only been dating for a few months when Verna Nell informed him she was pregnant and it was his. In a place like Kinston, and with a family like ours, a young man didn't just up and get a girl pregnant and then walk away. Every young lady's daddy had a bullet reserved in his shotgun for knuckleheads like that.

"Oh, great!" said Granddaddy Pressly, all happy, after he heard the news. His congratulations were sincere, because he knew what was coming next. "When are y'all getting married?"

So, at nineteen, Dad married Verna Nell Cox, who was just sixteen, because it was the proper thing to do. There was a child on the way that needed to bear his name. But proper as it may have been, it still wasn't reason enough for Dad to turn his back on true love. He didn't stop seeing Lacy, though they were respectful enough to carry on ever so discreetly.

Verna Nell wasn't stone-cold stupid; she had a hunch something was still going on between Lacy and my dad. She even sent some of her guy friends out to follow her new husband and confirm those suspicions. If not for the sake of love, then for the sake of their unborn baby, she wanted the marriage to be for real and to work out, so Verna Nell did what so many women do when confronted with their husband's infidelity—nothing. She kept her cool, and her man, because in the end it was actually Lacy who walked away.

"J. L.," Lacy told my dad, "we have got to stop this. It's not right. You're married, and your wife's about to have a baby.

This is ridiculous." My dad, bless his confused little heart, was shattered. But that was that; Lacy had put her foot down. A few months passed, and though it was hard, the two of them stayed away from each other. Dad heard that she'd started dating again. He figured that what he and Lacy shared was fully in their past now, that every day she was successfully erasing another piece of him. Soon he'd be nothing more than a faint memory, the hint of something that might have been.

Then one day Lacy came to him and said she needed to talk. He knew that it was over between them and there was no going back, but a part of him hadn't completely let go. He couldn't help but hope she'd come to tell him that the door was still open, that if he ever decided to walk through it, she'd be waiting on the other side. Unfortunately, it wasn't exactly the announcement she ended up making.

"J. L.," Lacy said, her mouth shifting back and forth between a nervous frown and an unsteady smile, "I'm pregnant." Dad's heart dropped into his stomach. He couldn't believe what he was hearing. What was he going to do? Two women pregnant within months of each other!?! By him! What were people going to think? To say?

"I do love you," he reassured Lacy, "and you know I want to be with you. I'll do everything I can to take care of you and the baby, but I'm married and I can't really think of making any moves, not until the baby I'm having with Verna Nell is born." Lacy looked awfully hurt, as though she had been waiting for him to say something else, to do something else, anything other than what he'd said and done. Nevertheless, she told him that she understood. What else could she do? Circumstances were what they were, and there was no getting around that.

Duke Pemberton was the man Lacy had started seeing after she and my dad broke up. Duke was a good guy, the classic fallback boyfriend, and he knew it, wore it like a mask on his face. He suffered from that distinct, painfully visible sadness people feel when they know that they are the second choice, the consolation prize, that there is someone their sweetheart loves more, wants more, and probably always will.

At a graduation party that year, Duke walked up to my dad, all serious-like. "There's something I want to say to you." Dad knew that it had to be about Lacy. After all, the two of them didn't have any other business between them. Dad guessed that Duke, knowing his place in the pecking order, wanted to reclaim some of his masculinity and insulted pride by reading Dad the riot act and telling him to stay away from Lacy. It was to be expected, so Dad waited for Duke to speak his peace.

"I just want you to know," Duke began, "that the baby's mine, not yours."

"What?" Dad asked. Duke repeated what he'd said. Dad thought about it for some time before he said anything else one way or the other, and after weighing everything, he decided that Duke was most likely telling the truth. Lacy *had* started dating Duke almost immediately after they'd broken up, and a few months *had* passed before she found out she was pregnant. All things being equal, the odds were stacking up in my dad's favor. The baby probably was really Duke's. Relieved as hell, Dad shook Duke's hand and wished him and Lacy the very best for a long, happy future. Unfortunately, that was not to be the case. Lacy and Duke broke up shortly after graduation. Not long after that, Dad heard she'd moved to Charlotte. Years later, he got word that she was living in Greenville. It's only about fifteen or twenty minutes away from Kinston, but it may as well be a whole day's drive, that's how far apart the two places really are. In all the snippets of gossip that got back to Dad, there was never any mention of the baby, and the few people who knew she'd even been pregnant hinted at a miscarriage.

Meanwhile, Verna Nell gave birth to my big brother, J. L. Jr. She and Dad stayed married for three very long, unfulfilling years before finally agreeing to go their separate ways.

The union between Uncle Ezra and the man he brought back with him from San Francisco didn't last either. That didn't dampen his spirits for long; he bounced right back and found his Mr. Right, the man my cousins and I grew up calling Uncle Lyle. After the initial shock of Uncle Ezra's "coming out" wore off, the family slowly came to terms with the fact that they couldn't turn their backs on their love for him any more than he could turn his back on his love for Uncle Lyle. And so it was: they accepted Uncle Ezra the way he was—all except my dad. It took him a little longer to come around.

Uncle Ezra was a hairdresser, a beautician, just like his mama. And, just like Grandmamma Pressly, he had a salon in his place, where he used to see clients. He also worked, doing hair, on the weekends and in the evenings, at the Caswell Center, North Carolina's oldest residential facility for people with mental retardation. Uncle Lyle worked there, too. It's where they first met and fell in love. Like Uncle Ezra, Uncle Lyle was tall and thin and good-looking, but he had sandy-blond hair and big brown eyes. I remember that he drove a champagne-colored Pulsar. I couldn't wait to grow up so I could own a car like that. Little did I know that Pulsars wouldn't even exist by the time I either got my driver's license or could rub two nickels together to buy one of my own.

Uncle Ezra and Uncle Lyle had two cocker spaniels, Delilah and Deacon. They used to breed them and give away the puppies—all of which had biblical names—to family and friends. Those men were truly religious and God-fearing. They attended church every Sunday and lived exemplary lives. They were kind, good-humored, and gentle men. The only thing anybody could fault them for was the love they shared.

While Uncle Ezra was on the job at the Caswell Center, one of the residents bit him, hard. It broke the skin, and from what I heard, the wound bled quite a bit. Uncle Ezra didn't pay that incident any mind. He patched himself up with some witch hazel and a Band-Aid, and went right on working. At a place like Caswell, things like that were tolerated and understood as par for the course. It was nothing to make any noise about. Several weeks later, though, Uncle Ezra came down with a severe mystery illness. He was told by the doctor that he had hepatitis C, and everybody assumed that he'd contracted the virus when he was bitten.

The treatment they gave him wasn't very effective, because he seemed to get worse, not better. Also, his symptoms were increasing, and they weren't totally consistent with a hepatitis C diagnosis. Uncle Ezra got so sick he had to be hospitalized. Grandmamma Pressly thought he had leukemia, and seeing as how, more often than not, she believed herself to be right, she made no bones about sharing that sound medical opinion with everybody, including Uncle Ezra's real doctor. As always, some of the family members agreed with Grandmamma, but most of them placed their faith in what the men who'd been to medical school said, this being such a grave situation and all. They were all nervous, and nobody really knew what to think. The one and only thing that they could all agree on was that if Uncle Ezra didn't get on a treatment regimen his body could respond to, it would only be a matter of time.

"Two weeks, tops," the doctor told Uncle Ezra before he checked him out of the hospital and sent him home to die. There was no way Grandmamma was gonna sit around helplessly and just watch one of her kids wither away like that. She may not have been a doctor, but she knew she had the one drug that nobody in a white coat with a framed degree on his wall could write a prescription for—love. And she administered it to Uncle Ezra in regular doses. She rubbed it into his skin like ointment whenever she held him, washed it over him with the warm cloth that she used to bathe him. She mixed it into the meals she prepared and delivered to him every morning, afternoon, and night, that good ole country cooking that she patiently fed to Uncle Ezra, in much the same way she used to when he was a baby.

At first, Uncle Ezra couldn't keep anything down, but Grandmamma wouldn't give up. She kept on cooking for him, filling up those teaspoons with food and holding them in front of his trembling lips.

"Come on now," she'd coax him, "just one more for Mama."

The two weeks that Uncle Ezra had been given by the doctors flew by, but instead of wasting away and dying, like they had predicted, he got stronger and started putting on a few pounds. He got healthy enough to get out of bed, feed, bathe, and dress himself. Soon, he was even able to return to work.

Love is, indeed, the strongest of all medicines. Uncle Ezra wasn't the only one who made a turnaround. Nearly losing his brother had a profound effect on J. L. Pressly. It didn't matter much to him anymore whether Uncle Ezra was with a man, a woman, or by himself, just as long as he was alive and well.

Uncle Ezra's recovery baffled his doctors. They didn't know what to think. He kept getting better and better until it got so you couldn't even tell that anything had ever been wrong with him. And he stayed that way for nearly a year, but then the remission ended and his illness returned, with what seemed like a vengeance. His decline was rapid. All the weight that Grandmamma had worked so hard to help him gain just melted off of him. It left everybody at a loss. They were right back where they started, doing battle against the unknown.

One day I was at Granddaddy and Grandmamma Presslys' house, sitting out in the gazebo with my dad's older sister, Aunt Careen. It was in the mid-1980s. We were devouring the latest issue of *People* magazine. She flipped the page we'd finished reading and on the left side of the new page was the acronym

AIDS, written really big in red block capital letters. On the right side of the page were all the symptoms associated with the disease. They were similar to those of hepatitis C. Aunt Careen had this shocked look on her face. At the time, AIDS wasn't yet a disease that people were familiar with.

"Oh my God," Aunt Careen cried out. "I think this is what my brother's got." She showed Grandmamma Pressly the article right away. The two of them were certain that this illness they were reading about in *People* magazine and the illness that Uncle Ezra had were one and the same. They took the magazine to his doctors, who read it and said they'd look into the matter. Within days, Uncle Ezra's diagnosis was changed. He had AIDS.

My dad owned a forest-green wood-paneled station wagon. During the time that Uncle Ezra was hospitalized because of AIDS-related complications, Dad must have taken up residence in that vehicle. He drove from work to home to the hospital and then back again. He visited his brother every single day, without exception, and stayed in his room until well after visiting hours were over. Getting him to leave Uncle Ezra's side was a near-impossible feat. Dad loved his little brother more than anything. They had always been close, but now there was something else, a new and unspoken element of their relationship. Dad was never able to live down what he'd done to his brother all those years ago. Uncle Ezra had never held it against Dad, but he didn't have to. Dad did that for him. Every evening before he left his brother's room, he would attempt to apologize.

"I'm sorry, Ezra. I am so, so sorry," Dad would say, fighting back tears. No matter how many times he said it, he still felt like it needed saying again.

"J. L., everything's fine," Uncle Ezra would remind Dad. "I know you love me and I know why you did that. You didn't know any better. Don't worry about it. Just be here for me now and forget about all that. Let's move forward, okay?"

So forward they moved, with Uncle Ezra virtually disappearing before everybody's eyes, going from his usual hundred and fifty-six pounds to under eighty pounds. He was just skin stretched tightly over bones. Nothing he owned fit him anymore. Not his clothes, not his jewelry or his shoes. Once he had shed them all, the only thing left for him to shed was life itself.

One night after work, Dad went to the hospital. He came a little later than usual because he had to make a couple of deliveries to customers. Dad walked into Uncle Ezra's hospital room and nobody was in there. The bed was all made up with clean, tight sheets. All the equipment had been put away. There wasn't a trace of Uncle Ezra. It was as if he'd never even been there.

"Excuse me," Dad called out to one of the nurses walking down the hall. "Was my brother moved to another room?" She looked at my dad, touched him lightly on the arm, and said, "I think you should call home. Your mother's been trying to get in touch with you." That's how Dad found out that his brother was gone. The call to Grandmamma Pressly was only a formality. There wasn't anything she could tell him that the now-vacant room which had once been Uncle Ezra's could not, and had not.

There was a ring that Uncle Ezra used to always wear. It was a man's ring of sturdy, solid gold with a single diamond in its center. Granddaddy Pressly had given it to Uncle Ezra some years back because he was the youngest. The Christmas after Uncle Ezra died, Dad unwrapped one of his gifts and inside the box was that ring.

"It belongs to you," his parents told him, "because you're the baby now." Dad placed the ring in the palm of his hand, closed his fingers over it, and made a fist. He brought the fist to his chest and he thought of Uncle Ezra, and he wept.

The awesome thing about life is that no matter what wrong you've done, it always gives you an opportunity to redeem yourself. You may be too stubborn to take that opportunity, or you may be too waist-deep in self-righteousness to even recognize it as what it is. Yet and still, the moment will come, and it will continue to come back in different ways, until . . . until . . . Just until.

The older Grandmamma Pressly got, the more she turned into a hermit. She didn't want to be anyplace other than her home. When she and Granddaddy Pressly bought their house, it was in one of the nicest areas in town—one of the nicest white areas, to be more specific. Over the years, that changed. It gradually became a black neighborhood. My grandmamma may have had her prejudices, but "white flight" wasn't in her life plan. She didn't care who moved in next door, not that she was pulling out the welcome wagon or baking any cakes for her new neighbors, but nothing and nobody was going to drive her away from her home.

The neighborhood surrounding Rochelle, the middle school that bore her family's name, also changed and became predominantly black. A ghetto, really, if you factor in class. It was as if Grandmamma Pressly's world was being cruelly reversed on her. Whereas she was once young and cute and able, by virtue of her race and class, to separate herself from an entire section of society, she was now old and crotchety and had become a virtual poster-child for integration. If the irony of it all was clear to her, she never let on. As far as she was concerned, her Kinston hadn't changed one iota, so she stayed put, refused to ever leave that house, the place where she had sustained her marriage and raised all her children. She even let one of her sons take over her river house, that's how adamant she was about having one place, and only that one place, be her home.

Actually, there were two river houses, located side by side, which had been in our family for over thirty years. One belonged to my parents, and the other, after Grandmamma Pressly let it go, belonged to my dad's older brother, Uncle Pruitt, and his wife, Aunt Francine, Madison and Gayle's parents. They were our little getaway spots, right on the water, in a town that was curiously called Oriental. Well, I thought it was curious because I'd never seen one Asian person in it, and there was no evidence of any other connection to the Orient.

Oriental, which was not far from Dawson's Creek—the *real* Dawson's Creek—was about a half hour from Kinston. During my freshman year in high school, my mom drove me out to the river house for one of our planned weekends up there. The first thing I noticed when we arrived was that there were all these unfamiliar cars parked outside.

"What's going on, Mom? Whose cars are these?"

"I don't know," she told me. She said it in a strangely nonchalant way that let me know she did know. We got out of the car and started walking toward the house. I was trailing behind her, sulking and being all dramatic in that classic teenager way.

"I need you to go inside and sit with me," Mom said. The last thing in the world I wanted to do was sit, trapped, in a room with my mother and the group of strangers who owned those parked cars, but it wasn't as if I had much of a choice.

Inside, there were some adults. Among them was a woman who, at first blush, looked an awful lot like Junior's mom, Verna Nell, but wasn't. There was a boy there, who looked to be around twenty-three or so, the same age as my brother, Junior. I swear, that boy was a spitting image of Uncle Ezra. He had the same everything—eyes, nose, teeth, hair. It was as if my Uncle Ezra had come back to life twenty years younger. I didn't understand what was going on, but I could not stop staring at him.

"Jaime," Mom called to me. "Let's go out for a walk on the dock."

"What for?" I shot back.

"Jaime," she muttered harshly under her breath. She was right beside me then, with her chin just above my shoulder. "Please, just shut your mouth and come with me." I obliged, but the instant we got far enough away from the house for me to safely cause a scene, you'd better believe I did.

"What the hell is going on in there, Mom? And what's all this about taking some stupid walk with you? What if I don't want to go? I mean, what do you want from me? Just tell me. Say it!"

"Jaime Elizabeth Pressly, you are so damned rude. Everything has to be your way, huh?" She shook her head and glared at me. "You want me to tell you, I'll tell you. That's your brother in there. He's six months younger than Junior." I stopped listening for a second to do the arithmetic. In my know-it-all adolescent mind, it didn't add up. *How does that work?* I thought.

"You have a son?" I asked, hesitantly. "I swear, he doesn't look anything like you."

"No," she exhaled. I could tell I was pushing her close to the edge of her patience. "He is not my son. Now, if you don't mind, would you please take a walk on the dock with me so we can talk?" Humbled by the reminder that my ignorance was far greater than my knowledge, I followed and I listened.

It turned out that when Lacy, my dad's old girlfriend, moved to Charlotte, it was to live in a home for unwed mothers. She carried her pregnancy to term, had her baby, and then gave him up for adoption. Afterward, she moved to Greenville and tried, unsuccessfully, to put the event in her past and go on with her life. She never had any other children and couldn't get her mind off the one she had given away. So she went through a child-search program and found him, her son. Duke Pemberton, trying to be a stand-up guy for his girl, had led my father to believe that the baby was not my dad's. But that baby was, and is, my dad's son. Suddenly, I had gained a half-brother, who was the same age as my other half-brother.

Raymond Rawlins is his name, and it wasn't only his looks that stirred up Uncle Ezra's spirit in our hearts. Raymond, who'd been adopted by a wonderful family in Charlotte, was a hairdresser by trade. He laughed like Uncle Ezra or, better said, like a Pressly—deep and loud and full of movement. And Raymond was gay. It was as if the heavens had given Dad his baby brother back—as his son. This was Dad's opportunity for full redemption. Thankfully, before Uncle Ezra's death, Dad had been given a chance to show his brother what was truly in his heart, beyond the fear, beyond the artificial boundaries that had been drawn by history and society's hatred. But Dad had only just begun; Uncle Ezra's death had come way too soon. Now, it seemed that fate was giving Dad yet another chance, and after the loss he had suffered, the countless days and months and years of missing his baby brother, of wishing that he had it to do all over again, after all that, you'd better believe that my father, J. L. Pressly, was surely not about to let this opportunity pass him by.

escape

Two houses down from mine, there was a humongous Southern magnolia tree. To my child-eyes, it looked like the biggest bush you'd ever seen, and it seemed to be as ancient as all time, completely overgrown and super-super tall, with branches jutting out like a million arms. There were thick, dark, emerald leaves around the outside of it, and they were garnished with gigantic flowers, blossoms so wide, creamy white, and shiny, they almost looked plastic.

That tree was like the eighth world wonder. You could actually part open the branches and walk inside. We used to play in there—me, Ruthie Hathaway, Madison, and Gayle. The three of them were the only kids I really hung out with.

Madison and Gayle lived around the corner. When we were

still in elementary school, I would ride my bike over there every day after classes. Madison was a year older than Gayle and me. She was bigger, too, tall and lanky. And she was smart, real smart and real practical, the kind of person that stands awfully close to people's idea of perfect. But she couldn't spell worth a damn and every chance we got we teased her to tears about that one fault.

Gayle was about the same height as me, but she eventually grew up to be the tallest of us all. She was thicker in those days, having not yet shed the remainder of her baby fat. Gayle was ballsy, had a lot of spunk and nerve, but she was also prissy and sophisticated, a different breed of tomboy—coloring outside the lines, yes, but ever so delicately. I was a tomboy, too, so she and I were alike in that way, but that was probably the only way. I didn't even look all that much like her, like either of them. Facially, they favored their mama; they had brown eyes and brown hair, which they wore in the same sensible bob style. My hair was long, blond, and, on enough occasions, untamed. I was the black sheep of the family, a free-spirited wild child. Ruthie Hathaway was the only one in our little town who really got that; and what she didn't get about me, she just let be, which is why she was my best friend.

When any, or all, of the four of us were together—Ruthie, Madison, Gayle, and me—our favorite game was hide-and-seek. One of us would place a hand tightly over her eyes or turn her back square against the wind while the others slid and skidded and kicked up dust trying to find the perfect place to hide, to run for cover so covert that couldn't nobody find us. Weren't too many places like that in the neighborhood, suitable for hiding and whatnot, so we would recycle the same seven locations and pray the one we'd chosen would be the least obvious to the person whose turn it was to seek as soon as she'd finished counting to twenty-Mississippi and called out, "Ready or not, here I come."

One of those supposedly ideal places was the small brick house directly across the street from Madison and Gayle's. It was blank, thoroughly empty, and had been since the old blue-haired lady who used to live in it passed away.

"That's 'cause her spirit's still floatin' 'round up in there. Ain't settled yet," I once overheard a grown-up saying. It was Charlene Haymaker, one of the big talkers in the town. She was full of it, admonitions and advice, none of which nobody needed or asked for, but got anyway whenever Miss Charlene was around. "Anybody who moves in," she'd said to my mother, "had better be ready to do battle with the dead."

Kids like creepy. They like it in books, on television, and at the movies. They even like it in the stories that other people tell, the kind of stories that give you the heebie-jeebies, but they definitely don't have as much tolerance for creepy when it's up close and personal, in their own lives. We were so scared by the possibility of coming face-to-face with a real ghost, we never went inside that house. Our explorations were restricted to the exterior, mainly the back area, where the woods were. Lots and lots of tall pine trees, as hovering and imposing as a group of hungry men after a long day's labor. We would go deep into those woods and lose ourselves in the many nooks and crannies and crevices. But I swear, even out there, I could sometimes feel a presence, like there was an extra set of eyes and pair of ears next to mine taking in every rustle and snap from the falling twigs and passing squirrels. It was easy to be still and invisible in those woods; we were too busy bracing ourselves against primordial fear to make any noise.

That huge magnolia tree was another location at the top of our short list. It was cozy and mysterious inside there, a whole other world, like stepping into your own little forest, except without the spooky, haunted feeling that you get when you're in the thick of the woods. Everything outside just fell away—people's voices and footsteps, the sounds of cars driving by. Those big ole leaves miraculously blocked every bit of it out, left you with nothing but your thoughts and the sound and rhythm of your own breathing. It was comforting, a great escape.

There were days, especially after I'd started middle school, when even though I wasn't playing hide-and-seek with Ruthie, Madison, and Gayle, I would go on inside there and stand underneath the shade of that magnolia tree, just let myself disappear. I could stay there for hours, or what felt like hours, daydreaming of all kinds of things while inhaling the light citrus scent of those alabaster flowers, or thumbing my way slowly through one of my magazines, usually *Teen* or *YM*. Sometimes I'd get so caught up in the fantasies I was having, so lost in the moment of another time and place, that when I came out from being under those leaves, I was startled to see my neighborhood again. Startled and disappointed. As ridiculous as it may seem, a part of me always kind of expected to walk out into a whole new town. I guess that's what they call "wishful thinking."

It wasn't a secret that I wanted to leave Kinston. My parents were well aware of that fact. Not that I knew where I wanted to be, mind you, but I was surely set on the idea that anyplace else was better than where I was. It's a complicated situation to explain, because I did love Kinston well enough, but I was also beginning to learn that love and like don't necessarily have a whole lot to do with each other. And hard as I tried, I simply could not bring myself to like it there.

Being different in a place where everybody tries real hard to look the same and act the same can eventually take its toll. Elementary school wasn't so bad, because Madison, Gayle, and Ruthie were there with me, though Madison was always a grade higher than us and had a different circle of friends. Our school, Northwest, which only went up to the third grade, was a feeder for C. H. Bynum, another Lenoir County public school, where students went for the fourth and fifth grades. After Madison and Gayle had each finished their time at Northwest, they transferred to the Arendell Parrot Academy, a private school where many of the well-off residents sent their kids.

Ruthie made the switch with me to Bynum. We were already tight, but that day-in and day-out of full-time, exclusive companionship made us feel more like sisters than anything else. A couple of people even told us that we looked like sisters, and it pleased us to no end, though we knew that was a stretch. We couldn't have ever been any more than a few pounds apart, and we always stood eye-to-eye, though Ruthie's were brown and mine were blue. Our complexions were around the same fair shade, but during the summer she freckled and tanned easily and that curly brown hair of hers lightened into a sandy blond.

Our time at Bynum didn't just cement our friendship, it set our unfavorable status as nonconformists permanently in stone. For our entire lives, Ruthie and I had felt free to be ourselves, without stopping to consider or care about what other people thought. You can do that when you're really young, because individual identity is either irrelevant or forgivable. Little children tend to be inclusive by nature. Everybody's content to sit in their seats with the rest of the class, reciting the capitals of the fifty states and the names of the two hundred and six bones in the human body, or to drag the first classmate in sight to play dodgeball and pat-a-cake with them at recess. But that changed once we started at our new school. The kids got cliquish and mean, and they started following the unwritten rules of some imaginary book of behavior. It got even worse when, after fifth grade, we had to switch again and start attending Rochelle Middle School. By then, our pituitary glands had got to working and puberty was in full swing. Fads and favorites became the order of the day. If you weren't friends with a certain person or didn't wear certain clothes, then you weren't worth knowing.

"Hi Ruthie. Hi Jaime," a gang of girls would squeal sarcastically as they walked past us in the hallway. Then you'd hear them snickering as they turned their heads to have another look at us so they could gather up some more grease and gristle for the frying. Those girls were part of the grand clique, a mini-colony, and Clarissa Weatherford was their queen bee. They all had big bangs and badly permed hair, those extra-long, nasty-looking poodle curls, and they wore tight Jordache jeans, lace-trimmed fold-down socks, and two-toned Keds. They'd contact each other the night before school to coordinate their outfits. The first call would come from Clarissa and the phone tree would work its way down from there.

"I'm thinking red and white," she'd say, and the next morning, we'd be swimming in it—pretty much everyone except Ruthie, in her loose, potato-sack shirts and Birkenstocks, and me, in my Duck Head shorts and loafers. Even the boys took part in the wacky wardrobe madness, because, naturally, the king of their personality cult was none other than Shelby Barksdale, boyfriend of Clarissa Weatherford.

It was disgusting. They were like royalty, our own middle-school version of Charles and Diana. He was the star athlete, a real cutie-pie, and Clarissa was the smartest girl in school, ultra-uppity and put together, the first one to fill out and start wearing a bra. She hand-picked her groupies and allowed them to take turns at being her "bestest buddy." One week it'd be Arlene Kinchelow, another week it'd be Constance Doggett or Jessica Scroggins, and so on and so forth. Ruthie and I, of course, were never on that rotation. They scrunched their noses up tight at us, like we had BO coming from the armpits.

"Can you believe what Clarissa and Arlene have on?" Ruthie would lean into me and giggle each morning. Her laughter was like poison ivy; it'd spread itself clear across her body, turning her cheeks, arms, and neck all warm and rosy, then it'd leap onto my skin and do the same. Before I knew it, I'd be giggling uncontrollably right along with her. It helped to ease the pain of alienation.

Seeing Ruthie every day was like waking up and looking out the window to find the sun blazing against the sky. It's an occurrence you just take for granted because you can't possibly imagine the alternative. Ruthie had moved a couple of times since elementary school, but she always lived right around one corner or another from me, never so far that I couldn't skip or pedal myself over to her place to spend time. Whenever I ran away from home, I went straight to her house.

"I'm leaving, going away forever," I would announce in a huff to my parents, slinging a stuffed backpack over my shoulder. "If anybody needs me, I'll be at Ruthie's."

I imagined that she'd forever be by my side, with the two of us taking turns as each other's shadow, each other's shield. Then, at the end of seventh grade, Ruthie decided she wasn't going to return to Rochelle. She enrolled in Arendell Parrot Academy, the school that Madison and Gayle were attending. In preparation for her new beginning, she spent that summer hanging out with her soon-to-be classmates. And that left me with no one.

I believe we choose our parents. I believe that our souls, unborn as they are, propel our moms and dads together to create a physical body for us to inhabit while we are alive. I believe we choose these specific people not only for their ability to teach and guide us, but for our ability to teach and guide them.

My mother never so much as told me directly, but I think she understood my desire to leave long before I even fixed my mouth to say the words. Whether she sensed it intuitively or simply felt it in the heaviness of the air that followed me from room to room, I can't say. I think it's more than likely she saw it in my eyes. Maybe every time she looked into them, she saw a reflection of herself, and recognized her own desperate need to flee. In fact, I'm all but sure that's it. That's why she worked so tirelessly and went to such extreme lengths to provide me with all the makings of an idyllic childhood.

All the kids in Kinston, even persnickety Clarissa, loved, loved, loved them some Andrea Pressly! And, of course, being that she was *my* mama, I loved her the most. She was the proverbial Kool-Aid mom, the one with the homemade treats and the medicinal hugs that could just patch you right up. She was a trained dancer, and became the choreographer for the town's performing arts department. When I was eight, she opened her own dance school, Studio 86. It was where all the little girls took their ballet, tap, and jazz classes. Andrea Pressly was the mom they all wished they had, the one they could talk to about anything, come and bawl their eyes out on her shoulder.

Madison, Gayle, and I were enterprising children. We formed ourselves a club that we called Girls Unlimited. It was our big money-making venture. When school let out for the summer, we organized a girls' camp that was held during business hours. We put together these different games and activities, supplied snacks and refreshments. We'd charge an entry fee of fifty cents per person and then we'd charge twenty-five cents for each game. Nobody else's mom would let them host the camp at their house, but my mother didn't mind having a handful of kids running around all day, so every summer we held it at my place. One after the other, those girls would walk in through our front door, their pockets full of quarters. Madison, Gayle, and I raked in a lot of dough.

Most weekends, Mom would take Ruthie and me to the river house in Oriental. We would have picnics, and go for rides on the boat. If Madison and Gayle were also up at their river house, which was right next door to ours, it would be an all-out party.

The childhood that Mom envisioned and made every effort to fashion for me contained everything, emotionally and materialistically, that her own childhood did not. She was born and raised in Grifton, North Carolina, which is about thirteen miles from Kinston. It covers roughly two square miles of land and only about two thousand people live there, so it's more of a village, a little village, like a hamlet. It's such a small place that when people talk about it, they couple it in the same breath with Ayden, another neighboring village, which, at two and one-third square miles and forty-seven hundred people is a wee bit larger. "Ayden-Grifton" is what people call that area.

Ayden is best known for gifting the world with Loonis McGlohon, the composer and jazz pianist, and for hosting the Annual Collard Festival, during which hundreds of people compete to see who can eat the largest mess of greens within a thirty-minute span of time. Grifton, on the other hand, is renowned for its Annual Shad Festival, which is more about attracting visitors to view the exhibits and participate in the arts and crafts than promoting the consumption of that little bony fish, which is abundant in the local waters.

Mom's mother, my Grandmamma Lynch, was a quiet woman who kept to herself. Mom's father, my Granddaddy Lynch, was an alcoholic. He drowned himself in booze and, as a result, also drowned whatever love and happiness his family could have made in their home, or found in each other. Their daughters threw themselves fully into extracurricular activities as a means of avoiding their parents and the problems that greeted them at home. For Mom, it was dance. For her sister, Julia, it was art. She became a painter.

In the pictures of my mother, when she was younger, you can see there was a strength about her that stood cautiously alongside all that sweetness. She's always been petite, five foot four, with a typical dancer's body—shapely thighs, hard-muscled calves, flat abdomen, and a small, almost imperceptible chest. There is a soft beauty to her face, too, the smooth complexion and the mousy, elbow-length brown hair, but those eyes . . . those wide blue eyes. They said all that needed to be heard. There was a hunger in them, a yearning. It was rumored that every one of those young men in Ayden-Grifton was keener on finding a way to drown in those eyes than fishing for hickory shad in Contentnea Creek.

Dance was going to be my mother's one-way ticket out of life in Ayden-Grifton. She was usually too busy practicing relevés, jetés, and pirouettes to be bothered with boyfriends, but when Norvell, a shy aspiring musician from the well-regarded Webster family asked her out, she reluctantly agreed. Instead of taking her to Haddock's or Sklight or any of the other usual spots in Ayden-Grifton, Norvell slid Mom into the front seat of his banana-yellow Plymouth Barracuda and drove on into the city. They went to Snoopy's, a pizza parlor in Kinston.

As soon as they walked in, Norvell saw somebody he knew, a girl named Liddie Valentine. Mom and Norvell were seated at a table. After they'd studied the menu and ordered their food, Norvell went over to say hello to Liddie. Mom didn't mind waiting for Norvell, but when he and Liddie proceeded to talk for a length of time that went well past reasonable and pushed right on into rude, she got up, went over there, and told him their date was over. Norvell, showing that he was not the honorable gentleman he was rumored to be, turned his back on my mother and left with Liddie. Mom returned to her seat and started eating her meal.

J. L. Pressly, my father, was at Snoopy's that night as well. He saw Mom when she walked in with Norvell and had to do a double take, she was so pretty. He couldn't take his eyes off her, so he watched as Norvell left her all alone to go make time with another woman. He watched as she waited, bored out of her wits. He witnessed the whole blow-by-blow, the way Norvell casually abandoned her, and the way she kept her composure and continued on with her evening, all by her lonesome. J. L. Pressly was not one to let a golden opportunity pass him by. He went over and introduced himself to Mom, sat down across from her, and smooth-talked his way into her good graces. The development of that relationship—marriage and, eventually, me—should not require further narration.

There were times when I used to walk in on my mother while she was sitting on the sofa or at the dining table, doing nothing in particular, just staring off into space. She'd have a look on her face that would make me pause, but only for a second or two, because the young are self-centered and focused primarily on their own concerns.

I can still remember that look, though. It wasn't exactly resignation or surrender, but it was close enough to pass. And I've put enough pieces together now to know that it was the look of a woman I had never met. No, she wasn't yet a woman, she was a young lady, the same one captured in those old photographs: Andrea Lynch, the dancer with those piercing blue eyes, the ones that craved something beyond the camera's scope, maybe even beyond her own scope. Those eyes, full of the desire for something more, those were the very same eyes that she passed on to me, her daughter. No wonder she knew.

If I hadn't been sent away that summer before eighth grade, I think I would have killed myself from too much crying. No lie. My mother or father would have come into my room and found me asphyxiated, laid flat out on my bed like a dead cockroach. As soon as I found out that Ruthie wasn't coming back to Rochelle, my life was over. I just wanted to be put out of my misery.

"Please send me to boarding school," I would beg each night. "I promise I'll get good grades. Please just send me away." When my parents refused, I'd start wailing, thinking of the long, lonely summer ahead of me and the days that would follow it, the days when I would have to walk down the hallways of that school by myself with Clarissa, Arlene, Jessica, and all the other girls passing me by wearing their culottes and button-down, washable-silk, neon-green shirts, saying, "Hi Jaime," in those phony, syrupy-sweet voices.

Technically, Ruthie and I were still friends, best friends. She still lived around the corner from me, but in a way, she was already gone; she had already moved into the world of Parrot Academy, a world that I didn't belong in. Instead of riding my bike down to her house to spend my days, I'd take my magazines and go sit under the magnolia tree. I'd flip through the pages and look at the models in the advertisements. Most of them were girls my age, skinny as broomsticks, and not all of them were that pretty. Some were gangly and funny-looking, hadn't yet grown into their features. And some were average, plain as half of the girls going to school at Rochelle.

"Well, she's not any better-looking than me," I'd sneer as I flipped a page. It had always been my dream to someday have my picture featured in a magazine. I figured that it would happen after I'd become a big, famous movie star, which was another dream of mine. But the more I looked at those magazines, the more I wondered why I should wait until then. I could do this now, I convinced myself. Sometimes, when I came out from under the magnolia tree, I would pretend that I was in Hollywood and the street in front of me was Sunset Boulevard, and the trees that lined it were palm, not pine or dogwood.

One day, as I was heading out for my usual spot under the magnolia tree, with my magazines clutched against my chest, my mother called me back into the house to tell me that I had to pack my bags.

"You wanted to go away, didn't you?" She laughed. "Well, now you're going."

Turned out I was going to be traveling to Charlotte to stay

with my aunt Careen and my uncle David for a couple of weeks. I couldn't believe my ears. I couldn't believe my luck. I held the magazines out and glanced at the cover of the one at the top of the stack. "Aunt Careen," I said to the model, as if that was her name. I closed my eyes and pulled the stack of magazines back toward me and held them tightly. "Thank you, God," I whispered. "Thank you, thank you, thank you," and went off to my room to get myself ready for the train ride.

Whenever Aunt Careen, my dad's older sister, and I were together, we'd pretend to be mother and daughter. She and her husband, Uncle David, have two sons, who they love dearly, but all my life I've occupied the space of the daughter Aunt Careen never had but always wanted. The Pressly genes are so bold and dominant that nobody who wasn't in the know could ever guess that I wasn't her natural-born child. Aside from all that, I was her child at heart. Whereas my mother was quiet, soft-spoken, and mild-mannered, Aunt Careen was brazen, a trailblazer who took no prisoners. She had also, at one time, been considered the black sheep of the family.

"I want to be a model," I told her as soon as I stepped off the train.

"So did I, when I was younger," she confided, without missing a beat to criticize or condemn what I'd said. "Hell, I'm still young. How about you and I go ahead and give it a try?" And that's the note we started my vacation on.

Within days, Aunt Careen had arranged for her photographer friend, Ray, to take pictures of us. After the pictures were developed, we went to an agency called Carolina Talents. We showed them my pictures, and Aunt Careen, dressed in her finest, struck some death-defying poses before pulling out her own pictures. They signed both of us on the spot and scheduled us to take more pictures the next day with their own photographer. It was an amazing shoot. We changed into at least a half-dozen outfits, pursed our lips, arched our backs, and threw ourselves into all kinds of diva positions while the man behind the lens just kept clicking away.

My time in Charlotte ended way too soon. But it had served a purpose far greater than the fun I had with Aunt Careen, and I did have fun. While I was there, I devised a plan—not foolproof, but feasible—to get me out of Kinston and away from Clarissa and her kind, the shortsighted, small-minded people who make life in a small town downright gloomy and unbearable.

When school started, the days I'd spent in Charlotte seemed so distant, like something I'd daydreamed while sitting underneath the magnolia tree, or staring out of my bedroom window at the sky, another one of my favorite pastimes. Ruthie and I had started hanging out again after school, but not as often as we used to. She had, indeed, managed to get away from the obnoxious mega-clique at my school, but only to discover that while the kids at Parrot Academy weren't the same as the kids at Rochelle, they did have their own power-elite system, and all that money only gave them more incentive to show off and act up.

Midway through the first semester of eighth grade, I got a package from Aunt Careen. Inside were all of the pictures I'd taken while I was in Charlotte, and a bunch of copies of the professional comp card that she'd made for me. There was one particular picture that everyone, especially the folks at the agency, had thought was extraordinary. It was a tight shot of me, dressed up in leopard-print sixties garb, looking very Brigitte Bardot-ish. In the photo, I look like I'm saluting someone—either that or searching for something over a horizon. *This is the one,* I thought. *This is the one.*

That weekend, I got on my bike and rode over to Ruthie's house. She was in the throes of a fight with her brother, Beau. He was a strange one, "touched," as my Grandmamma Pressly might have put it. He was fond of collecting vermin, nasty creepy-crawly insects, the stranger and uglier the better. He'd bring them into their house, drop them into the aquarium, and study them like he was some kind of freak scientist. Ugh!

"Help me out, Jaime," Ruthie screamed, as she was reaching to swat him in the head. The two of them were tangled up like they'd been playing a game of Twister. I guess Beau didn't realize I had come into the house, because he turned to look at me, and that gave Ruthie the advantage she needed. She knocked him over, broke free, and made for the door. We raced out of that house. Messing with my bike would have cost us precious time. I left it where it was and ran with Ruthie through the neighborhood, giggling and panting, until we got to my front porch.

"I want you to help me do something," I told her. We were buckled over, with our hands on our knees, taking in as much of the November air as our lungs could hold.

"All right," Ruthie exhaled. No questions asked.

"Wait here," I said and went inside. "Dad? Dad!" I found my father in the kitchen, with his head deep inside the refrigerator. "Dad, can I have ten dollars?"

"What for?" He pulled his head out, stood up, and closed the fridge door.

"I'm going to the mall with Ruthie. I wanna buy some stuff. Where's Mom?" Dad shrugged. He pulled his wallet out of his back pocket. Lately, my parents never seemed to be in the same room at the same time. It was almost like they were doing it on purpose, like they were trying to avoid each other. If Dad was in the bedroom, Mom would be in the kitchen. If Mom was in the kitchen, Dad would be out on the porch. I guessed it was probably just a very busy time for both of them. He pulled out a ten-dollar bill and handed it to me.

"Thanks," I said, and started running back out to Ruthie. Mom was with her. They were sitting on the porch swing, talking.

"Hey, Mom. We're going to the mall. You ready, Ruthie?"

"You girls want a ride?" Mom offered. We were going to have to walk back to Ruthie's house to get our bikes, and I didn't feel much like dealing with Beau and his evil mood. Ruthie and I went and leaned against the station wagon. While we were waiting for Mom to go inside and get the keys, I told Ruthie all about my plan.

In a weird kind of way, I guess you could say that magazines are a lot like television. You look at them for the people, to find out what they're wearing and what they're doing. They're like openings, glances, occasional opportunities to survey the other side. You can't help but compare the things in your life with what you see. I know that sounds like it could be a bad thing, like you're almost setting yourself up to feel inadequate because the average person doesn't have half of those glamorous items. But what's also there in that comparison is the vision of what you can be, and what you can do, if you're able to get yourself through that opening, or map out an alternative route to get to that other side.

I was never one to watch too much TV. Between school, gymnastics, dance, and hanging out with Ruthie and my cousins, I didn't stay in the house long enough. What I did used to do was read every magazine I could get my hands on, like *Teen, Seventeen, Mademoiselle, YM, Glamour,* and *Sassy.* I'd take them with me wherever I went. In the backs of those magazines were ads, about the size of business cards, for model searches. You had to send in a dollar to the address that was listed, and they would send you back an application. That was my big plan: to become a model. A long shot, huh? But hey, nothing ventured, nothing gained. I figured I stood about as good a chance as anybody else. Why not try?

When Ruthie and I went to the mall, I changed that money my dad gave me into ten singles. We came back home, went up to my room, and started addressing envelopes and licking them shut. I spent every last one of those dollars asking for applications. A couple weeks later, they came in; one then another then another. I filled them out, attached the picture I had chosen, and dropped them in the mail. The only thing left to do was wait.

So wait I did. The holidays came and went. I checked the mailbox every day after school. There was a constant stream of bills and letters. Never anything for me, unless you count Christmas cards addressed to the whole family. I didn't stop waiting, but it slowly became less of an active thing.

A new year was upon us, 1991, and my main resolution that year—brought on, no doubt, by the excitement of entering into those searches—was to be happy, only that. In order to reach that goal, I had to get rid of all the obstacles that stood between me and it. This meant either a change in attitude or a change in approach, depending on the exact obstacle. When it came to the obstacle of Clarissa Weatherford, I decided it'd be best to use a combination of both. And I had a plan—not foolproof, but feasible.

I invited Clarissa over to my house to spend the night. My aim was to get on her good side. I had no interest in joining her clique or becoming one of her lackeys. I was content being myself and minding my own business, which, for reasons unknown to me, caused her to hate me. But I knew that there had to be an in-between, a way that she and I could get along, and I was going to find it. That night, I pulled out all the stops. I oozed kindness like it was ketchup going on a hot dog. I read her excerpts from my personal journal, my innermost thoughts. Of course, I had written those portions specifically for that purpose, hoping they'd get her to see me in a better light and change her mind about me.

"That is stupid," she told me after I was done reading. "And look, you totally misspelled Arlene's name." I couldn't win for losing. Instead of making my life easier, I'd made it worse. When Monday rolled around, everybody knew what I'd read to Clarissa from my journal. She'd spent the weekend burning up the phone tree, calling the girls to give them an earful. Her boyfriend, Shelby, did his part and spread the news to the boys. For a solid month, I walked around that school feeling like I had a KICK ME sign taped to my back. I missed having Ruthie there at Rochelle. There wasn't nothing I wouldn't have given to hear her giggling in those hallways again.

Because I'd dropped those applications and photos in the mail, I'd naturally expected that the model searches would also get in touch with me through the mail. Nothing came by way of letter, but a month before summer vacation, they started calling. They left messages on the machine saying that they had received my picture and they felt I had tremendous potential to be a professional model. Then each of them went on to talk about the program they offered, which would provide me with the proper training I needed to move forward in that career. They were very expensive programs, which my parents weren't prepared to pay for. Once those so-called scouts figured that out, nearly all the calls stopped, except the ones from a guy named Jonathan LaPeer.

Every few weeks, throughout the summer, he'd call. A couple

of times when I got home from hanging out in the neighborhood with Ruthie or Madison and Gayle, I'd hear a message
from him on the machine. My cousins were still going to Parrot Academy, but Ruthie had decided that her first year there
would be her last. She was coming back to public school. Since
Rochelle ended with the eighth grade, that fall we'd be starting
ninth grade together at Kinston High School.

It was a quiet summer, especially inside our home. On the
surface, everything was normal. Mom, Dad, and I ate together,
we talked; we did all the regular stuff we usually did. It was like
we were going through the motions, but there was a hollowness
to it. There was an important part missing. Something had definitely changed, and I knew it, though I couldn't quite put my
finger on what it was.

At the end of that summer, Jonathan LaPeer called and got a
live person on the phone.

"I'm with ICMS, the International Cover Model Search," he
explained to my mother. "Jaime sent us a picture. She's got her
hands over her eyes and it looks like she's searching for something."

"Mm-hmm . . ." Mom was listening, but I could tell from the
way she was half-squinting one eye and raising up the brow on
the other eye she was a little suspicious.

"I would love to use that picture in our ad, and I would really
love to bring her out here to California to do a shoot with us."

"Um, let me think about that, talk it over with her father, and
we'll get back to you."

"Well?" I asked, after she'd hung up the receiver. I'd been

standing close to her, close enough to hear both sides of the conversation.

"I don't know, Jaime," Mom started, shaking her head. "It could be a scam. We'll think about it."

I knew better than to pester my parents too much, or else it would backfire. Thankfully, the first few weeks at Kinston High kept me distracted. There were a million new faces and names to remember. The sophomore girls were intense. Talk about cliquey. They made Clarissa and her gang look like a Brownie troop. But this was high school, the big time. Ruthie and I were small pickings for them; they left us alone.

I tried out for the JV cheerleading squad and got in. Those eleven years of dance and gymnastics training paid off. We were expected to be better than good, because Kinston had the best athletic department in the state. Our soccer team was number one, and Jerry Stackhouse was on the basketball team, leading the school to victory. Things were looking up for me. I wasn't as unhappy as I had been, but thoughts of leaving still lingered in my mind.

"Mrs. Pressly?" my mom heard when she answered the phone. It was October. I remember because some of the leaves on the trees had started turning and folks in the neighborhood were already putting out pumpkins and other Halloween decorations.

"Jonathan LaPeer again, with ICMS. I was calling to follow up on our last conversation. Like I said, we'd like to bring Jaime out here for a photo shoot with our photographers."

"How do I know this isn't a scam?" she came right out and asked.

"We're a legitimate company," he assured her. "We've been in the industry for quite a while. Listen, I'll pay for your plane tickets, and put you up in a hotel. I'll pay for everything. Please come." Both of my parents, in their own individual ways, were protective of me, but they were each also pretty supportive of my dreams, ambitions, and (though I didn't see them that way at the time) half-baked schemes. Mom accepted Jonathan LaPeer's offer, but with a big ole heap of hesitation.

Aunt Careen came with Mom and me to California that November. I'd never been anyplace like that before. Not that I had a lot to measure it against. Really, I'd never been anyplace. Kinston was beautiful in a way I'd come to consider ordinary. Southern California was beautiful in a way that was too good to be true, the wondrous kind of landscape you stumble into while you're dreaming, full of vibrant colors, shiny cars, people with deep tans and clean shoes. There was no polyester. Or old ladies with bouffant hairdos. There weren't any old ladies at all. Not a wrinkle or liver spot in sight. Everybody looked young, even the ones that you knew were older. It wasn't at all like the make-believe California I used to see when I stepped outside of that magnolia tree.

Jonathan LaPeer wasn't at all what I thought he'd be, either. He wasn't stuffy or scary or unapproachable. He was handsome, average height, in his late thirties or early forties, with a full head of hair that was prematurely gray, just a normal guy with glasses. He had large framed photos on his walls of the models that they'd discovered through their search and the magazines they'd been featured in. I tried to picture myself in some of those photos, and I wondered if one day there'd ever be a photo of me on those walls.

Over the first three days, I shot with seven photographers. Each one had a different set of looks he was trying to get, a different style of giving direction. It was exhausting but fun, though not as much fun as I'd had while shooting in Charlotte with Aunt Careen. After the shoots, Mom, Aunt Careen, and I would go sightseeing and people-watching, taking in what we could of California before returning to the hotel to eat dinner and go to sleep. On our last night there, I was lying in bed with my mother, facing her back. Her hair was sprawled on the bed; some of it was stuck in the tiny space between our two pillows. Aunt Careen was fast asleep on the other bed in the room.

"Mom?" I whispered. "I really like it out here. I really wanna do this. I wanna move to California." I'd been hinting at that since we stepped off the plane.

"I know," she said. "I gotta think about it, think things through. There's a lot that I would have to give up."

"Well, I'm gonna come anyway," I told her. "I know I can do this. I can make money *and* go to school."

"If you come out here, Jaime, I'm coming with you." She sounded tired, too tired to fuss. I closed my eyes, pulled the blanket and sheet a little higher so they covered my shoulders. As I tried to drift off, I replayed what she'd said, and something struck me.

"Mom?" I opened my eyes and nudged her shoulder with my hand. "If we come out here, would Dad come with us?" I could hear her taking a breath. She blew it out softly. It was almost a sigh.

"I dunno, honey. Probably not." A tingling sensation traveled down my neck and into my arms, stopped in my wrists and stayed there. I could feel my pulse, my heartbeat.

"How would that work?" I asked, wishing she would turn around and look at me.

"We'd figure something out. A schedule, so that he could come visit you or you could go visit him." Suddenly, a series of images from the past two years flashed through my mind. Her in one room, him in another room, the forced smiles, the thick silences. It was coming together now, each image falling into place. How could I have not seen it before? How could I have not known? I propped myself up on my right elbow.

"What do you mean *I* could go visit him? You'd go visit him too, wouldn't you?" I'm not sure why I asked that question. In a way, it had already been answered. Maybe I just needed to actually hear the words, to have my mother say them out loud. I waited. The tingling sensation was gone. Now, I was growing numb.

"No, honey," she said finally. "I wouldn't." I put my head back down on the pillow, closed my eyes, and sucked in my cheeks, hard, to keep from crying.

My parents separated. A couple of weeks after we got back from California, Mom and I moved to Fox Run, a community of town houses in another part of Kinston. I'd never lived anywhere else except the home that we'd once shared with my father, and it felt odd. The new place was fine, but it was just that, a place. It felt foreign and temporary, like a hotel. I hadn't realized what a big part of my life my old neighborhood was, how it defined everything I did. I missed riding my bike over to Ruthie's, or Madison and Gayle's. I even missed that haunted brick house with the woods behind it, where we used to hide. The four of us had long outgrown playing hide and seek, and somebody had moved into the house anyway, so their yard was off-limits to us. I especially missed that ole magnolia tree, though lately I hadn't taken to sitting there much.

My mother was going through her own emotional changes. Dad was the first and only real relationship she'd ever had. She'd been with him for twenty-one years, since she was eighteen. She'd moved to Kinston to be with him. His town had become her town; his family had become her family. She'd spent years investing herself in a marriage and an identity that she thought would last forever. Divorce was still controversial in our corner of the world, especially a divorce between Andrea and J. L. Pressly. The sorrow and disillusionment my mom was dealing with inside was hard enough. Having to then put on a brave face to contend with the people she ran into outside must have only made it worse, people like Charlene Haymaker, who made everybody's private business a matter of public record. Mom was distraught. She was preoccupied and distracted most of the time, probably trying to find her own answer to the question that all of us were now asking: "What next?"

After the holidays, during the first week of 1992, Jonathan

LaPeer called us again. He said he loved the pictures from the photo shoots I had while we were in California. He'd even shown them to the editor at *Teen*, who also loved them, so much that she wanted to arrange a photo shoot with me for the cover of the magazine.

"Because you've never worked before," Jonathan told me, "they're going to be shooting three other girls who they're also considering for the same job. Whichever one of you guys is able to give them the shot they're looking for will get the cover."

That February, Mom and I flew back out to California for five days so that I could do the photo shoot. I found California even more refreshing than I had the first time. It was a clean slate, and I clung to the idea of having a fresh start in a new city. It had a far greater appeal than the reality of what we were doing, which was trying to make a fresh start in an old town. Once again, I brought up the subject of moving to California, and again, my mother said she'd think about it.

Within days of our return, Jonathan called to tell us that I had been chosen for the cover of *Teen* magazine. I took it as a sign that the heavens were conspiring to grant me my wish, and that was the whole point of the plan—to leave Kinston.

Every beginning signals the end of something else. My school life was insane. I was trying to pack the entire four-year high school experience—Sadie Hawkins, homecoming, prom, parties, boyfriends, cheerleading, you name it—into the ninth grade, because I didn't know what was ahead, what life had in store for me. All around me things were coming to an end, making their transition from one phase of being to another, going through a metamorphosis. I was also in the midst of making that journey.

After we found out about the *Teen* magazine cover, I sat down with my mother to have a talk.

"When school's out," I told her, "I'm moving to California. Now, are you gonna come with me or not?" I was staring her straight in the face. She knew I was serious, that I'd really do it. I was through with waiting.

Think about it: a mother and her fourteen-year-old daughter, standing at the edge of a precipice, each searching for an escape, a way out of the circumstances confining them. The daughter, headstrong and full of urgency, says, "Let's just take the leap."

How many women do you know who would put their future in the hands of their teenager? How many would say to their daughter, like my mother said to me, "All right. Let's do it."

place

"Dude" is a Southern California word—like, totally. It was the first of many I picked up soon after our arrival. And a good thing, too, because it came in handy whenever I hung out with Brayden Scott and Joaquin Turner, who, I guess you could say, were the first real friends I made when we got there. I spent the better part of that summer with them at the beach, which, as it turned out, was only a ten-minute drive away.

I met the boys through Brayden's sister, Brianna, who worked at the complex where our new apartment was located. She was the one who showed the vacant units to all the prospective tenants and tended to the administrative stuff like accepting rental applications and processing paperwork. This meant she knew pretty much everything about everybody who lived there, including my mom and me.

Joaquin Turner was like a character right out of a beach movie. He had long golden-blond hair, a deep tan, smoked a large amount of weed on a regular basis, and drove an early 1970s VW bus. It was two-toned, red bottom/white top, a classic that Joaquin and his father had restored. They'd rebuilt the engine, changed the tires and rims, and slapped several coats of acrylic urethane enamel on it. It was their pet project, something they chose so they could do it together. Joaquin's family was like that, really cool and very close. But they seemed like characters out of a movie, too: hippies, flower children, holdouts of another era, still wearing peace symbols, tie-dyed T-shirts, and John Lennon glasses.

Joaquin was an incredible artist, the last of a dying breed. He could draw and paint anything at all, but his passion was psychedelic art—you know, as in Grateful Dead paraphernalia, the kind of art that seems like it's best appreciated while under the influence of a mind-altering substance.

Brayden Scott was Joaquin's best friend, a fellow stoner. He was also a conceited little son of a gun. He was on the short side, had sandy-brown, overgrown, beach-bum hair and skin so tan you could tell that it was already a warm shade of olive even before the sun had had its go at it, making it darker. Brayden was definitely cute, but he thought way more of himself than that. He thought he was God's gift to women. Or, more specifically, to me, since being around me was probably the closest he got to spending time with a real live woman that entire summer, not counting his sister and his mama, naturally.

Whenever the three of us hung out, Brayden would find a way to sidle up to me and say, "Dude, you and I should dump this loser and make it a one-on one." Joaquin was the mellow kind. He took it in stride. He'd chuckle, shake his head a few times, and then look at me as if to say, *Is this guy serious or what?* This made me feel all the more comfortable around him, around both of them.

Brayden and Joaquin weren't like any kids I'd ever met in North Carolina. I found them fascinating and I liked being in their company. They became my unofficial tour guides, except what they showed me wasn't part of the usual "Welcome to California" package, replete with landmarks and sights intended for visitors. They yanked me into their lives and gave me direct access to some of the inner worlds of this place I now called home.

Late June of 1992, that's when my mom and I arrived in Costa Mesa. I got there first, about a week and a half before her, because I flew and she drove, kept her foot on the pedal clear across the entire country in a U-Haul filled to capacity with every knickknack and stitch of clothing we owned. Hitched to the back of that U-Haul was our Nissan Maxima. Some mornings I'd wake up and I couldn't believe that we had actually done it. Mom and I had actually left North Carolina, made our great escape.

It was as if, for years and years, our lives had been going along in the same ole same ole and then suddenly something snapped, setting off a chain reaction of life-changing events. First was Ruthie Hathaway going to Parrot Academy and leaving me to fend for myself at Rochelle. Next was my trip to Aunt Careen's, having her take me to get pictures and then being signed with Carolina Talents. After that, it was me applying to each and every one of those model searches and having one come through that wasn't a scam. Then it was being flown to California for a series of test shoots and then it was my parents' marriage blowing up right in their hands, like a bad science experiment. But that wasn't the end of it. There was more, so much more.

June 1992 was also the month that my face appeared on the cover of *Teen* magazine. Had I been back in Kinston, I'd have probably stolen more than a few moments of glory watching the faces of people like Clarissa Weatherford and Arlene Kinchelow freeze up, right there in the summer heat, and crack into a million little pieces after seeing me, the one they'd undervalued and underestimated, smiling at them on thick, glossy paper from every newsstand and drugstore shelf. But I wasn't in Kinston; I was in Costa Mesa, too caught up in the whole business of acclimating to my surroundings to really celebrate that undeniable victory.

A month later, on July 30, 1992, I turned fifteen. I didn't think much of it when it happened, because where I'm from, fifteen isn't one of those big-deal birthdays that serve as a significant rite of passage. It was only later, months later, I found out from the Latino kids I met in school that to some people fifteen is a big deal, a really big deal. It's your *quinciñera,* the Spanish-speaking cultures' equivalent to our American "sweet sixteen." A young girl's coming of age, entering the first utterly confusing phase of womanhood.

Obviously, I'm not Latino, and I didn't have a claim—not then, anyway—to any part of that culture, but this concept of *quinciñera* was meaningful to me all the same. I had just closed one chapter of my life, and "womanhood" seemed just as good a title as any other to write on the blank page of this new chapter I was beginning.

"Culture shock" is too harsh a term to describe what I went through the first several months after our move. During my visits to California, I had been shuttled between our hotels, Jonathan LaPeer's office, and the photographers' studios. Most of what I'd seen was through windshields and windows, from the perspective of a passing car. Still, I'd fallen in love instantly. It'd left me desperate for more.

Now I had that and I couldn't help but to be floored by all the differences between Kinston, North Carolina, and Costa Mesa, California. There was so much I hadn't noticed when I'd been there before. For a while I couldn't see or experience anything new without first measuring it against all that had once been familiar, expected. When you've only known one group of people, one type of architecture and landscape, one dialect of the language, and then you encounter another, it leaves you lost in a dizzying game of comparison between here and there, between these and those.

The street signs in Kinston were small and green, with

names like "Herritage," "King," "Queen," and "Caswell" written on them. The ones in Costa Mesa were as huge as placards,
with writing large enough to read from a distance. They had
names like "El Modena," "Cabrillo," "Santiago," and "Antigua,"
words I could hardly pronounce, written in huge, chalk-white
letters.

Whereas I used to be able to walk around the corner to my
cousins Gayle and Madison's house, or around the other corner to Ruthie Hathaway's, there was nowhere to walk to in Costa
Mesa. The city blocks were long, and besides, walking wasn't
something that Californians did a whole lot. They drove, and
even then they rarely drove for any serious length of time on the
streets—the "surface roads," as they were called. People used
freeways, even for traveling short distances.

In the mornings, after Joaquin and Brayden picked me up,
we'd drive onto the 55 Freeway and sail past the handful of ex-
its that stood between us and Newport Beach, where the freeway came to an unceremonious end. The city of Newport Beach
neighbored Costa Mesa, but was far more affluent. The air there
smelled of both salt and money.

Joaquin would park, and the three of us would get out of the
VW and walk toward the water. We'd have to trudge through
what seemed like miles and miles and miles of sand.

In North Carolina, it barely took a hop, skip, and a jump to
get from the street to the sea. That's because years of erosion
had eaten away at the coastline. The beaches may not have been
as sprawling, but they offered capes and sounds, like Cape Hat-

teras and Pamlico Sound. They offered egrets and seashells by the dozens.

From what I could see, besides a pier, harbor, jetty, and spectacular waves for surfing, one of the main attractions of Newport Beach was skin. I couldn't believe people wore bathing suits that covered up so little. Standing next to those girls in their string bikinis, my one-piece may as well have been a habit. And the makeup! Who knew that girls wore makeup—and sometimes jewelry—to go hang out at the beach? I sure as hell didn't.

When I wasn't rolling my eyes at Brayden's pathetic flirtations or trying to decipher Joaquin's latest kaleidoscopic masterpiece, I'd gape at the girls working the boardwalk like it was a runway. "Who *are* they? What kind of girl would walk around in something like that?" I would wonder, without having the slightest idea that soon enough I would know.

The night before my first day at Kinston High, Ruthie Hathaway and I stayed on the phone forever, discussing our wardrobes, our classes. We went over every detail we could consider, right down to the exact moment we would meet each other in front of the doors of that building to make our grand entrance into high school.

Since kids from other middle schools in the area would also be attending Kinston High, there was a whole population of students we didn't know. But at the end of the day, in a small town, you know everybody, whether you realize it or not. There's really no such thing as a stranger. You may not know somebody's name, but chances are your life is already somehow linked to theirs. They may belong to the same church as you; your parents or grandparents might go way back to before you were born.

But that was all in the past now. The night before my first day at Costa Mesa High, I realized that I wouldn't know a single soul there. Brayden and Joaquin attended Newport Beach High, and though I'd waved and said "hello" to the few people they'd introduced me to during our times together at the beach, I hadn't gotten to know anybody else.

I was going to be walking into a school full of strangers. Real strangers. There wouldn't be anybody there who'd heard of the Presslys, taken dance classes from my mom, or had their hair done by Grandmamma Pressly. For the first time in my life, I was going to be anonymous. I didn't get a wink of sleep. I kept tossing and turning, thinking about what that might be like, how it would feel to be just another face in the crowd. But in the end, how I imagined it was not how it turned out at all.

One piece of information that Brianna Scott knew about me and readily shared with Brayden and Joaquin was that I'd been on the cover of *Teen* magazine. I was aware that the boys knew, but they never really talked about it. Not with me, but apparently they did with other people. And those other people passed the information along to their friends, too.

When I got to school, everybody had seen that issue of *Teen* and they knew who I was. They even had a nickname for me— "model chick"—and that's how they referred to me. No matter how many times I'd introduce myself, nobody called me by my name. It was, "Hey, model chick." I saw them pointing at me and I could hear them whispering to each other, "That's the model chick." It was kinda hilariously ironic, because on that particular day, there's no way I could have met anybody's expectation of what a model should look like.

The outfit I chose to wear might have gone over well in Kinston but, much to my horror, in Costa Mesa, it could have easily placed me on Mr. Blackwell's notorious list of fashion fiascos. Guess? was a popular designer label at the time, so I had on a pair of black jeans from their line. I wore a long-sleeved, button-down black-and-white flannel plaid shirt on top, and I had on a pair of black boots. *Plaid? Flannel? Boots?* What was I thinking? It was September in Southern California, which meant it was blazing hot, and there I was, looking like I was fixing to walk into a snowstorm.

None of the other girls were dressed that way. None of the other girls were dressed, period. It was more like they were in various stages of undress. I wore more clothes in my dance classes than these girls wore to school. Back home, cheerleading uniforms were the closest we came to being racy. But here, in this school, the girls were wearing short-cropped tops with padded bras that pushed their boobs up to their necks. They wore them with Dolphin shorts and flip-flops or sandals. And good God, the makeup. These were the boardwalk girls, the ones I'd seen at the beach all summer. Everybody was so painted up they almost looked plastic. Little plastic Barbie dolls, with big blond bangs that had been hairsprayed to a crisp. Well, everybody who was white.

The Latina girls wore their hair in long ponytails. They used Tres Flores pomade to keep the front shiny and slicked back, but they'd keep the back full and crinkly. They wore a lot of makeup too, but they didn't apply it the same way the white girls did. It seemed as though they were especially fond of pencils and liner. They shaved their natural eyebrows and used a black pencil to draw thin fake ones on. Their mascara was thick and clumpy, and they always extended the eyeliner past the edge of their eyes. Even though the lipsticks they wore were brightly colored, they lined their lips with black or dark-brown pencil, so the contrast was stark.

Those were the main racial groups, white and Hispanic. There was also a fair number of Asian-Americans, though not as many in comparison. There were even fewer African-Americans, and if there were any Native Americans, I never met them. What we had in Kinston was blacks, whites, and Native Americans, in that order. When I was living there, we didn't have a huge number of Hispanic people, though now, of course, they are a growing segment of the population. But back then, I had never even spent time with or around them. I didn't know the difference between a Mexican and a Puerto Rican. That would all change before the end of my first year at Costa Mesa High; I would go on to meet and get to know people from nearly every Spanish-speaking country on the globe.

I would also meet different types of people—the surfer types, like Brayden and Joaquin, the gang-banger types, the potheads, and the taggers. I would eventually learn how to identify each of them by what they wore or didn't wear. Like the taggers. They wore baggy clothes, and when they walked, you could hear the spray cans jiggling in their backpacks.

The gang-bangers weren't that difficult to distinguish either. There were about eight gangs at Costa Mesa High, and I caught on fast how to figure out who was with which gang. Each gang had specific colors that they wore, certain tattoos etched into their arms and necks, and they communicated using their own set of hand symbols and gestures.

But that would all come later. On that first day, walking the halls in my boots and flannel shirt, being called "model chick," the only thing I knew was that it felt like I had fallen into one of Joaquin's paintings. It was bizarre and beautiful at the same time. That's what made it so welcoming. It was the sort of place where you could easily get lost, or be found.

friends

When you're the new kid at a school, the first day is like a game of Russian roulette. You say "hi" to everybody, and most of them say "hi" back. You're anxious to make an ally, someone to ease your transition and help you negotiate your way through the maze. So anxious that you go running, like a pet-store puppy, to the first person who smiles, pats at an empty spot by their side, and says, "Come. Come sit here with me."

Granted, it might just be the rescue you needed. You might just have found the friend who will stick by you for the rest of your life. Or it could be that you've committed social suicide, buddied up with a nerd, a loser, and forever assigned yourself a seat at the sorriest table in the cafeteria.

It was lunchtime, and I was standing by myself, surveying my surroundings, trying to quickly get a sense of the social pecking order. I didn't want to end up with a bunch of weirdos, but I also didn't want people to see me just standing there all friendless, looking like Little Orphan Annie, because, well, then they'd think *I* was a weirdo.

I saw a group of girls who seemed harmlessly ordinary, and I decided to walk up to them and introduce myself. But just when I was about to take a step in their direction, another group of about five girls came walking toward me.

"Hi," one of them said. "You're that model chick, right?" Before I could answer, another one held her hand out to me.

She said, "I'm Lily. Lily Benson. We know Brayden. He told us about you." I was relieved. If they were friends with Brayden Scott then they had to be all right. The other girls introduced themselves, too: Heather, Isabel, Wendy, and Vivica. Standing just behind them were two other girls. I couldn't tell if they were part of the group or if they were just eavesdropping. They were staring right at us and whispering comments to each other.

"Are they with you guys?" I asked.

"Yeah," the girls all said without turning around to look.

"That's Skyla and Sabina," Heather told me.

"Don't worry about them," Lily added.

"When did you move here?" Vivica wanted to know.

"Do you have any brothers?" Isabel chimed in.

I didn't know where to start. The girls were standing in a tight semicircle around me, each asking her question, hoping that it would be the one that was sharp enough to break the ice so that we could warm up to each other. I laughed, out of sheer nervousness and also because I was happy to have landed safely in their company.

"Well," I said. "My mom and I moved out here from North Carolina in—"

Just then, Skyla, one of the girls who had been lurking behind the group, elbowed her way to the front. She was standing, arms akimbo, with an attitude. "All I gotta say," Skyla snarled, "is that you'd better fucking stay away from my boyfriend." It was like a scene right out of the movie *Mean Girls*. I barely knew where the bathrooms were in the school and here was some scrawny five-foot gremlin giving me grief about a boy.

For a moment, I had a sinking feeling in my stomach, just like the ones I used to get when Clarissa Weatherford and her posse of persnicketies would stick it to Ruthie and me. I felt like I had just popped a whole grape down my throat and it was freefalling through my large intestine. I swallowed, took a deep breath, and asked, "Who's your boyfriend?" What else was I supposed to say?

"Stone Glazer," she told me. She said it as if I should have already known, as if he were a presidential candidate whose name was plastered all over billboards and bumper stickers and I was just pretending to be clueless. But I really didn't know.

I looked at the other girls to find out what was going on with them, whether this was actually some kind of ambush that they were all in on, an initiation joke at the new girl's expense. Lily gave me a grin that let me know that she, at least, had been sincere.

"Where in North Carolina?" she asked, kinda rolling her eyes and dismissing Skyla.

"I used to know somebody from North Carolina," Vivica said.

"Who? Claire?" Heather asked, rolling her eyes at Vivica. "She wasn't from North Carolina. She was from *South* Carolina."

"Same difference. It's close enough," Vivica told her. Then all of us, including Skyla, laughed at her. And just like that, I was in.

You know how in almost every public high school class, there's at least one kid in there who looks way too old to be with the others? It's usually a guy, and he's usually tall, with big, clunky feet, a few hairs on his chin, and a baritone voice. There was a guy like that in my sophomore history class. He'd been eyeballing me during that first class, acting like he wanted to come up and say something to me after the bell rang, but he didn't. He picked up his notebook and pencil and walked out the door.

On the second day of school, he and I walked into the class at the same time, damn near knocking each other over to get through the door frame. Embarrassed, I flashed him a few teeth to be friendly.

"Model chick, right?"

"My name's Jaime," I corrected him.

"Jaime," he repeated. "Stone." *Aaahhh,* I thought, while I was going to my seat. *That's Stone Glazer.* It still took a moment to sink in. Huh? I did a double take. *That* was Stone Glazer? Skyla's boyfriend? I bit my lip to keep from laughing. There is a God, I thought. How fitting for the little gremlin to be dating Tweedle Dumb.

I'd later discover that Stone wasn't actually dumb. He merely lacked the skills needed to pass tenth-grade history. He'd failed it at least once, and he was having another go at it so that the administration would let him graduate with the rest of his senior class. I'd also learn that on the first day, Stone had told his best friend, "Fat" Francis, he thought I was pretty, and "Fat" Francis—who was indeed pudgy, but was called that more because of his big, fat mouth than his big, fat butt—went and told Skyla, which is why she'd issued that warning to me.

But what was done was done, and I steered clear of Stone, especially then, because I didn't have all those details yet, and I didn't want any kind of trouble. I sat toward the back of the class and spent the whole period looking at the Latino boys. They called themselves *cholos*. I couldn't stop myself from staring at them. It wasn't so much a crush as it was a curiosity.

I was drop-jawed by their features, the brown skin, and the black, shoe-polish hair. I liked the way they spoke English—flawlessly in class, broken in the hallways, with a teeny-weeny accent that only came out when they said certain words. And the way they spoke Spanglish when they were talking to each other, or to their girls, the *cholas*, with their ponytails and long Elvira hair.

I even liked to hear their names, to practice the sound of them softly in my head, the way I did with the street names—Xavier, Francisco, Arturo, Diego. I especially liked the name

Jesus. I didn't know you could do that, name somebody Jesus. Nobody I knew in North Carolina would've been so bold. It seemed irreverent, almost taboo, like naming somebody God. But that's what drew me to it, to them. I wanted to know more about their culture.

Just before my mom and I left Kinston, we'd had a farewell party at our town house. My cousin Madison brought her boyfriend. He was a big baseball fan and he used to always wear his favorite team's cap. I guess at some point during that night he'd taken it off, because the next morning I found it on the couch, stuffed between two cushions. I probably should have given it back to him, but I didn't, and ever since then, it'd become my favorite cap and my favorite team.

After dressing so distastefully that first day, I showed up on the second day wearing a pair of shorts, a tank top, and that New York Yankees cap. I had a free period right after history and I'd noticed that some of the *cholos* who I'd just been in class with were hanging out in the parking lot. I went over to say "hi" and talk to them.

They were standing there in their white wife-beaters, black jeans, and Nike Cortez sneaks. Each of them had a red bandanna hanging out of their back pocket. I knew it meant they belonged to a gang, but that was the extent of my knowledge. I've never been one to fear what I don't know. That might be brave or it might be stupid, probably a combination of both, but to me the unknown was, well, unknown, so why be afraid of it? I walked up to those boys and greeted the ones I knew—that is, if hearing somebody's name called in class by the teacher counts as knowing them.

"Ah, model chick," Diego said.

"For crying out loud," I muttered under my breath, "is any-body ever gonna learn my name?" I made a mental note to kick Brayden and Joaquin's asses the next time I saw them. This was all their fault.

"Jaime," I said, for the umpteenth time that day. "My name is Jaime."

I stood in front of them and waited for somebody to say some-thing else. Nobody spoke. They all stared at something over my head. I looked up, thinking maybe a bird was about to poop on me or something, but there was nothing there, and then I real-ized they were staring at my cap.

"Yankees," I said, touching the visor part of it.

"You like Crips?" Diego asked. I could tell it was a serious question. He'd been leaning against a car, but he'd stood up straight to ask that, his eyes piercing right into mine. I didn't know what he meant. I thought it was some sort of slang for "cripple," a word I never use. It was such a strange question. Why would he want to know whether I liked handicapped people? What difference did it make to him? Nevertheless, I answered.

"I guess." I shrugged. "It depends on who they are."

"What???" Diego seemed pissed off with me. So did the other guys, who were now also standing at attention. They looked like they were following Diego's lead, at his back, waiting for what he would say or do next. I was sure that if he had walked away and snapped his fingers, they would have trailed behind him automatically, like hounds out for the hunt.

"Why does it matter whether or not I like crippled people?"
I asked. Over the years, one of the many sayings I heard my
Grandmamma Pressly say is that "God protects babies and
fools." And right then, there couldn't have been a bigger fool
than me, trying to start up a conversation with a bunch of gang
members while wearing a cap in a color that was the symbol of
their archrivals. Diego busted out laughing, and within seconds, the rest of his gang joined him. I laughed too, though
I didn't know what I had said or done that they'd found so
damned funny.

Things at home weren't perfect, but my mom and I were managing. She'd taken a job teaching ballroom dancing, which she
hated, hated, hated. Jonathan LaPeer had also given her a part-
time job as an administrative assistant at his model-search
company. She was grateful for the opportunity to earn extra
money, but she was way overqualified for a position like that. It
must have felt like a demotion in life, walking away from everything she'd spent her entire adulthood building and then having to start all over with nothing.

My dad had always done well for himself. He was a hard
worker, but out of the two of them, my mother was the one
who'd earned more. In order for us to move to Costa Mesa,
she'd sold her dance studio for far less than it was worth, because she'd wanted to preserve the integrity of the program
she'd created for the kids in Kinston, and now she was struggling to make ends meet.

I suppose when you're working that hard, you've got to take comfort wherever you find it. For my mom, that was next door. Our neighbor was a man named Richard Peterson. He was in his early forties, originally from New Jersey, with an accent to prove it, and he wore his hair in a mullet style. During the day, he worked in the commercial plumbing business; in the evenings, he spent time with my mother. The two of them started seeing each other a couple of days after she and I moved in. All right, maybe it didn't happen that quickly. Maybe it was more like a couple of weeks. Whatever amount of time it was, it sure felt like the blink of an eye.

I'd never imagined my mom being with anybody except my dad. The two of them being together forever was a given. They were my parents. It was a union I thought would always exist, like the one between my Grandmamma and Granddaddy Pressly. Grandmamma still loved him and considered him her husband even after he was dead and buried. And I can guarantee you, if there's a heaven, the two of them are there together, and she's working his last nerve, and he is loving every minute of that odd afterlife companionship.

But change was upon us, every which way we looked. As hard as it was for me to have my mother tell me she was going next door, and to see her straightening her blouse and using her hand to brush her hair out of her face in that special way a woman does when she's off to meet a man she's interested in, I looked the other way and prayed that this, too, would pass.

With kids, friendship can be as instant as a box of oatmeal, except instead of water, you add laughter and there you go; it's ready to be enjoyed by all. That's how it was with Heather, Isabel, Wendy, Vivica, Lily, and me. The six of us got along great. Skyla and Sabina weren't as fond of my presence, but they begrudgingly accepted me as part of their group.

Diego and his gang came to accept me, too, though not as one of them. They acknowledged me whenever they passed by me. "*Buenos dias,* model chick," they'd say, and tap the visor of my Yankees cap if I was wearing it. If they were hanging out and I was around, I'd go stand with them and join in their conversation. Turned out they liked hearing me speak as much as I liked hearing them. There weren't too many people there with Southern drawls, and I'd often say things—just ordinary words in ordinary sentences—that left them in stitches.

"Yo, say that again," Xavier would plead, with a tear skating down the side of his face. When he got to giggling, his eyes were quick to water.

"What?" I'd ask, purposely exaggerating my accent. "All I said was that those McDonald's biscuits aren't half as good as the ones they make at the Bojangles back home." Then they'd all crack up again. But it was hard to get annoyed, since I did similar things to them.

"What's that word you taught me the other day?" I'd ask Diego, even though I hadn't forgotten it. We'd go back and forth until I made him say it. One day it'd be *chingon,* the next, *cabrón.* It bugged the hell out of the *chola*s to see me with Diego and his gang. Whenever the *chola*s and I were together with the guys, they'd act as though they liked me. Whenever they were near me and the guys weren't around, they'd still smile, though not as hard, and they'd call me names in Spanish, crude and nasty names, not knowing that I understood every word because the boys had taught them to me.

During the second week of school, Vivica and Heather and the rest of the girls invited me to a party that coming weekend. Thankfully, it was around the corner from my apartment, so getting there wouldn't be a problem, since Mom and I no longer had a car; Mom's Nissan Maxima had become yet another casualty of the divorce.

By then, I'd already made some critical adjustments to my North Carolina sense of style. I had picked up several sticks of Wet n Wild lip gloss, extra-heavy mascara, and a few push-up bras. Since I couldn't afford a whole new wardrobe, I got creative and devised a way to mix, match, and wear my clothes so that I wouldn't stick out like a sore thumb. It was my first California party and I didn't want to embarrass myself.

On the night of the party, I called a cab. Since the car had been repossessed, our primary method of transportation, besides hoofing it and bumming rides, was public transportation, though Mom sometimes got rides from Richard Peterson, our next-door neighbor, her new boyfriend. Coming from Kinston, taking cabs wasn't a common practice for either of us. The night of the party was the first time I'd ever done it by myself. The only other time I'd taken a cab was when I was much younger and had traveled with my mom to New York. Back when I was a little kid, that process had seemed not so much complicated as sophisticated, an adult transaction. Now, when I was a young adult in Costa Mesa, it didn't feel that way at all. It was, in fact, pretty straightforward. I gave the cab driver an address and he dropped me off in front of the house where the party was taking place. No big deal . . . but I've gotta say that for only a few blocks, it was a really expensive ride.

I felt awkward walking in by myself, but once I stepped over the threshold and saw some familiar faces, it wasn't so bad. Inside, it smelled like weed and about ten different brands of perfume. I mingled until I ran into a few of the girls, my new friends. Wendy, Isabel, Lily, and I were standing around trying to talk to each other over the music when I spotted Skyla and Sabina. Skyla came and stood in front of me, really close. She was three sheets to the wind. I could smell the liquor on her before she started speaking. And her eyes were huge, swirling around in their sockets, like the way they draw them in cartoons after a character has been hit upside the head and begins to see stars.

"Listen," she slurred. "I'm really sorry about the way I was when we met. But I wanna ask you a favor." She was swaying slowly, like a tiny tree in a light breeze, trying to keep her balance.

"Okay, what?" Skyla took a sip of her drink and dropped her hand down so quickly to her side I thought she'd drop the glass, too. Then she looked up at me again with those swirly lollypop eyes.

"Okay, would you please go out with my boyfriend?" I scrunched up my face. Huh? After that threat she'd made the first day of school, I'd been staying far away from Stone, treating him like he had a communicable disease.

"What? No! I already told you, I'm not going to touch your boyfriend."

"No, no, no, no," she said. "Here's the thing." She put her free hand on my shoulder, leaned in even closer to me, and whispered, "See, I wanna go out with his friend Luke, and Stone wants to go out with you. It's okay, really."

Apparently, it was something Stone and Skyla had already discussed. They'd been dating exclusively for three years and they each wanted to know what it'd be like to be with someone else. Luke would be that someone else for Skyla, and I guess I was supposed to be it for Stone. It was too bizarre. Nothing good could come out of a situation like that, not for me. I wasn't having any part of that madness. I refused, told her "no" ten times in ten different ways, but she was hammered and she would not let it drop.

"Just think about it, okay?" I told her I would, so she'd leave me alone and let me enjoy the rest of the party—which she did, and which I did.

That encounter left me with a feeling of foreboding. Everything had been going so well at this new school, and now I was screwed. If I went out with Stone to appease Skyla, I'd be screwed. It wasn't like they were going to break up. And the point of going out with other people was not to sit and talk about the weather during the date. Something more would be expected. Then after they'd each finished experimenting, they'd get back together and I'd be—what?—screwed.

The other alternative wasn't any more appealing. If I continued to refuse, which I fully intended to, Skyla would never let me forget it. It'd stand in the way of us really becoming friends, something I'd hoped would happen over time as we got to know each other better. And if she and I weren't friends, it'd make it pretty difficult for me to remain as close with the other girls in the group, because they'd all been best friends since long before I entered the picture.

Why me? I wondered. I'd catch Stone stealing glances my way during history class. I'd been keeping my distance from him, but now I was extra careful. I didn't want to encourage him in any way. I was hoping that if I kept ignoring him, he'd stop liking me and choose another girl to have his experience with. Either that or else Skyla would forget.

No such luck. That Tuesday afternoon, she came up to me and asked if I'd thought about it like I promised I would. "I don't think it's a good idea," I explained. "I can't do it. I won't do it. I'm sure he's a nice guy, but I don't like him in that way." She said, "All right," but her eyes told me that I'd be punished for not playing along.

I was wrong. She didn't punish me. What Skyla did instead was talk Stone into calling me that night to ask me himself, hoping maybe he'd be able to soften me up or sweet-talk me into doing it. When Stone and I spoke, I gave him all the reasons I gave her why I didn't want to go out with him. He was a nice guy, and he seemed to understand and empathize with my predicament.

"Look," he told me before we hung up. "We don't have to really go out. We'll just tell her we're going to so she won't feel bad about going out with Luke. It's no big deal. Don't even worry about it."

Suddenly, I felt bad about having been so standoffish toward him. And I felt sorry for him, for being stuck in this deal he'd made with Skyla. It still wasn't enough to make me go out with Stone, but I did agree to go along with the ruse he'd invented.

I think all that worrying I'd been doing about that situation made me sick. By the following week, I had come down with something. I had a fever, my head hurt, and my body was achy all over. I tried to make it through as much of the day as possible, but I couldn't take it any longer. I had to go home and get in bed. I'd been given permission to sign myself out of school, so I went to the office to do just that.

As I was leaving the office, I ran into Stone.

"What's the matter?" he asked. I must have looked as bad as I felt. I told him I was calling it a day because I was sick. He and I had been talking to each other in history class a little here and there since the phone call. He told me he was on his way home, too. Because he was a senior, he had two free periods, and they were scheduled back-to-back at the end of the school day. He offered to give me a ride. I hadn't been looking forward to the long walk ahead of me, which was mostly uphill, so I was happy to hop into that car with him.

When we got to my place, Stone walked me up to my door to make sure I got in okay. We were standing outside talking, and, after a while, I started to feel light-headed, like I needed to sit down, so I opened the door and he came in with me. My mom was still at work. Stone and I were sitting together on the couch chatting and the next thing I knew, he was leaning over, kissing me. I pulled myself back, placed my palm against his chest, and gently pushed him away.

"I'm sick," I reminded him. "And on top of that, I don't want to do this."

"Let's just do it for Skyla," he whispered, leaning in toward me again.

"No. No way. I won't do this." I stood up. "You have to leave." When he was gone, I climbed into bed and fell into a long, heavy, Nyquil-induced sleep. By the time I woke up the next morning, the sun was shining and it all seemed like it had been nothing more than a bad dream.

When the shit hits the fan, the best place to be is in bed with the flu. I was out of school for two days, which was more than enough time for Stone to confide in his best friend, and for "Fat" Francis to break his promise to keep Stone's secret. He told Skyla what happened between Stone and me, embellishing a fact or two here and there for added effect. Instead of the real story, which was that Stone kissed Jaime, who immediately pulled away and then told him to get out, "Fat" Francis's spin was that Jaime took Stone to her place and she had sex with him. He turned it around so that I was the culprit, the one who had crossed an unforgivable line.

Being as sick as I was, I hadn't talked to anybody, so I didn't know that my name, which I had worked so hard to get everybody to say, was now mud. By Friday night, I was feeling better. I called the girls to find out what their plans were and if I could join them. I'd been cooped up for too long. I wanted to go out.

Nobody answered my calls, or returned the messages I left. I kept trying. Nothing. I tried all day on Saturday, too. Nothing. When I did reach a live person, like a parent or a sibling, they'd tell me to hold on, then they'd come back on the line a few minutes later and lie to me: "You just missed her," or "She's taking a shower right now."

Finally, on Sunday, I got hold of Lily. She was calm and pleasant, but I could hear that something was off. She told me what had gone on while I'd been under the covers shivering and sneezing. What she said brought me to tears. In that instant, the weight of everything I had been keeping at bay came crashing down. I missed my best friend, Ruthie, and my cousins, Madison and Gayle. I missed my dad, and my parents being together. I hated living in an apartment instead of a house with lots of room and a yard. I hated my mom being broke all the time. And I hated the idea of her dating or falling in love again, with Richard, the next-door neighbor, or anyone else.

I had a complete and total meltdown on the phone with Lily, not in words but in tears. I cried and cried and cried. She held on patiently until the sobs quieted down into sniffles. When I could talk again, I told her my side of things. She said she'd tell the other girls and get back to me.

"What'd they say?" I asked when she called back.

"You and I are cool," she said. "I want you to know that." I could feel a "but" coming, and I held my breath. "But the rest of the girls are gonna leave it up to Skyla." Leave it up to Skyla? The future of my friendships with five girls was in the hands of one person?

"You mean if Skyla decides she doesn't want to be my friend anymore none of them will be my friend either?"

"Um, I don't know," Lily said. She did know, but she was too nice to tell me that the answer was "yes."

I didn't go to school the next day. I wasn't sick; I was depressed. Lily came over that afternoon because she was worried about me.

"Everything'll work itself out," she insisted. "I'm sure it'll all be fine."

When I returned to school on Tuesday, I hung out the entire time with the *cholos*, learning new Spanish cuss words and letting them laugh at my accent. Theirs was a complex existence, full of bravado and violence, whether imagined or real. Still, it felt simpler than mine, because I wasn't in it. I was simply standing on the sidelines, which is right where I wanted to be.

Stone sat face-forward when we were in class. There were no more stolen glances. It would take him weeks before he could manage to speak to me again, but when he did, he apologized.

Lily, on the other hand, said "hi" whenever she saw me, and I waved back at her. The other girls were slow to come around, but they eventually did. They started saying "hello" to me before the week was out. Apparently, Skyla had decided that I wasn't going to be snubbed. I'd still be part of the group.

That Friday night, which was a little over a week from the day Stone had kissed me, they all came over to my apartment unannounced.

"We're going out," they said. There was a spot in Newport Beach that they wanted to check out. Brayden and Joaquin were going to be there, too. They wanted me to go with them, but in order to get in we had to be dressed up, so all of us were going to have to change clothes. They'd already rotated through each of the other girls' closet, so they asked me if I minded opening mine up to them.

I watched them while they were in my bedroom, pulling out my clothes and holding them up in front of themselves as they posed in the mirror. There were questions and giggles. There were hugs and jokes. They acted as if nothing bad had ever gone down between us. I realized that it was a dangerous game we were playing. Still, despite my fears, despite everything that had happened, I liked them, especially Lily. I didn't hold out any hope that this reconciliation would make it through the weekend, yet somehow I knew that if any of my relationships with those girls would last, it would be the one I had with Lily. I suspected that out of all of them she would be the person I'd call my friend forever.

emancipation

Yeah, whatever.

That pretty much summed up my feelings as a teenager on just about everything. I didn't give a damn; on the other hand, I cared too deeply. I liked being the center of attention; but then again, I wanted to crawl into a hole and be left alone. I lived in emotional states as extreme as the two geographical states I had called home. It was because that menacing messenger of puberty, the pituitary gland, was hard at work. Those hormones were shooting like fireworks inside my mind, making me crazy. They were doing a number on the rest of my body, too.

By the age of fifteen, I looked like I was in my twenties. I had the figure of a grown woman. Men in suits and ties, sitting in their cars at traffic lights, would blow their horns at me while I was walking down the street. I could walk into a bar and order a drink, no questions asked. Not that I did, mind you. Or walk into an eighteen-and-over club with a fake ID in my pocket and never be carded. Now that, I'll admit, I did do a few times. There were definitely benefits to looking older than I actually was. But there were also penalties.

Jane Ford, who was the editor of *Teen* magazine, decided that they couldn't use me anymore in their publication. "Our market is teenagers," she told me. "You've gotten too sexy for the magazine. I'm sorry." I'd been on the cover of *Teen,* and had done a few shoots for photos that ended up being featured on the inside pages. I'd convinced my mom to move us to California so that I could do more work for *Teen* and other magazines. I wanted to be a model, and, in the beginning, everyone had been so excited about my potential. But in the two years that had passed since my first photo shoot, I'd gone through a growth spurt and filled out faster than anybody, least of all me, could have expected. And now, I was out of a job.

Knowing how devastated I was by that news, Jonathan La-Peer, whose model-search company had "discovered" me and was now using me as a spokesperson, offered to submit me for a long-term assignment in Japan. If I were selected, he told my mom and me, I'd have to be legally emancipated. It was just a technicality, something I'd have to do in order to live on my own in a foreign country. We would have to petition the courts to declare me an emancipated minor, which meant that in the eyes of the law, I would be considered an adult. I'd have all the legal privileges and rights of an eighteen-year-old, even though I was fifteen.

Because of my parents' ongoing divorce, I was becoming more and more familiar with legal documents. I wasn't really happy with either of my parents at the time. I don't think any kid that's caught in the middle of a divorce is. It shakes your foundation, makes you question things you'd never even thought to consider before. You begin to pull away from whatever sacred image you'd had of your parents, the two individuals you've loved and admired most in your life, and see them as plain ole adults. Adults at war, with each other; adults in love, with other people.

One of the main things my father wanted in the divorce was me. He wanted me to come back to North Carolina and live with him. I knew because I'd read it, seen it with my own eyes, in the papers that had been mailed to our apartment. Richard, my mother's boyfriend, showed them to me. They were on the dining-room table.

"I thought you should see these," he said to me. "I thought you should know that your dad wants you back." So I looked, and there it was, sure enough, a request for custody.

I didn't want to go back to North Carolina, but that had nothing to do with not wanting to live with my dad. Even though I was mad at him and resented the part he was playing in everything that was going on, I loved my dad and I wished, more than anything, that there was a way for us to live together again, all of us. But there wasn't, because they weren't getting back together, and I wasn't going back to North Carolina.

Kinston was a part of my past now. It wasn't like I could click my heels and return to what had once been: living in that big house, riding my bike around the neighborhood. Sure, I'd been surrounded by a lot of love and happiness while I lived there, especially from my family. But I'd also been subjected to a lot of misery. I'd felt like a misfit.

When I used to sit under the magnolia tree, it was California that I'd dreamed of. It was modeling and acting that I'd dreamed of. So no, I wasn't going back to North Carolina. That decision had been made long ago. Not that I was particularly thrilled about living with my mother, either.

Her relationship with Richard had been getting more and more serious. Now it was more than going next door to see him, or spending the night at his apartment. He was always over at our place. I'd leave for school in the morning and he'd be there. I'd come home from school in the afternoon and he'd be there. I'd hoped that whatever was going on between them would end sooner rather than later, but it didn't look like that was going to happen.

I didn't like Richard. It wasn't like he'd ever done anything bad to me to cause that. He was nice enough, especially in the beginning. Boyfriends always start off being nice to the kids of their girlfriends. The only fault I found with him was that he was dating my mother. That, in my mind, was a huge one, as huge as the San Andreas. And it caused some pretty strong tremors in our household.

My father had a girlfriend, too, which I found equally disturbing. I didn't like her either, and for the same reasons. But the thing with her was that I didn't have to see her day in and day out. It was a classic case of out of sight, out of mind. I had the luxury of pretending she didn't exist.

School was the one thing that was going right. I had created my own little community. It was widely accepted that the group of six girls I spent the majority of my time with were the "it" group. By that, I mean they stood out. It was a large school, but everybody was aware of them, knew their names, and recognized their faces. They were popular, and by virtue of my closeness with them, I started to stand out too.

There were different levels of friendships within the group. I knew, for instance, that Sabina didn't care too much for me. I believe Skyla liked me, but only superficially. I was tight with the rest of them, but Lily had become my best friend.

My time in Kinston, and the brief falling out I'd had with the girls at Costa Mesa High, had taught me to be wary of cliques, and to not isolate myself within any one group. I retained my individuality and freely associated myself with various other people.

Costa Mesa High was riddled with gangs. At the time, it wasn't exactly the safest place on earth. Before the end of my first semester there I knew, and was on good terms with, a number of those gang members. They were unlikely friendships, but that made them all the more interesting and meaningful.

School was my refuge, my haven. When I got there, I didn't have to think about my mother, money problems, my father, the divorce, or Richard. And if I was thinking about any of that, there were people there, at school, who understood how I felt.

In many ways it seemed like the better and more stable my life at school got, the worse and more unstable my life outside of school became. Richard moved in with us. If I'd thought his constant presence in our apartment was an intrusion before, now I considered it an invasion. Not only was he in our home, he was in my life, trying to assume the role of an authority figure.

He was inserting himself in discussions on matters that concerned me, adding his two cents into decisions having to do with me. He wasn't just stepping into the role of my mother's partner, he was trying to step into the role of my parent. And it seemed as though I didn't have any say in the matter at all.

My response was to ignore him. I'd come home from school with my friends, and we'd disappear into my room and close the door. We'd turn on the radio and blast the sound. Then we'd sit on my bed and smoke cigarettes, blow rings of smoke out the window and talk about how our lives sucked.

The guy I was dating, Chris Zucker, was going through similar problems at his house, so he and I spent a large part of our time together commiserating. Chris was a real rebel, and I think that's initially what attracted me to him. Plus, he was smart, one of the smartest people I'd ever met. He lived with his mother and stepfather. Chris felt about his stepfather the way I felt about Richard, except with better reason. Chris's stepfather made it apparent to him that he was unwanted.

His real father had died as a result of police brutality. So for Chris, there was nowhere else to go. He had a well of anger in him, which he drew from so often he was sometimes drowning in it. I related to that well, to that anger. That's because I had my own, though maybe not as deep as Chris's. Being with Chris provided me shelter from all that, and I was grateful for it. We both were.

Another reprieve came in the form of a part-time job at Express, a clothing store not too far from our place. The extra cash came in handy. It saved me from having to ask my mother for money all the time. That's actually why I got the job. We were surviving, but barely. It hurt me to see my mother having to work as hard as she did at a job she hated so much, and I wanted to help, if only by eliminating the burden of always having to worry about giving me money to do the things I wanted to do. Since the work that I'd been getting from modeling had all but dried up, this seemed like the next best solution. An added bonus was that it gave me somewhere legitimate, other than home, to be for a chunk of time every weekend, which meant that I didn't have to be around Richard.

My father was adamantly opposed to my being emancipated. Even though at the end of the process I would be seen as a legal adult, I needed the permission of both parents in order to file the petition. His opposition to it only brought more conflict into our already strained relationship.

My mother was willing to sign the papers, because she knew that it wouldn't change anything. I reasoned and reasoned with my father, but he wouldn't give in. To him, it was more than a technicality. He told me that his girlfriend had researched it and he didn't feel comfortable relinquishing his rights as my legal guardian.

Years later, I would go over his words in my head and realize that he was only trying to tell me he wasn't ready to let his little girl go. He'd already lost me, in one sense, as a result of his separation from my mother. I was living thousands of miles away from him. And here I was asking him to prematurely release what little hold he had left on my life as a minor, as his daughter. But I didn't hear what he was really saying, I couldn't, not in the chaos of all that was being destroyed and reconstructed. I interpreted what he said to mean that he was intent on making me return to Kinston.

I was furious. I stewed for days, weeks, and then I reacted. I called my father and told him that I needed him to sign that petition. I explained that I needed to do this for work, my work as a model. The words that I've chosen in the writing of this—"told," "explained"—fail to convey the level of rage and disrespect I displayed in that conversation.

There are few choices I regret making, even those that I would not make if I had a chance to choose again. Our choices set us firmly on roads that lead us to other roads, which guide us to our destiny. Maybe speaking to my father as rudely as I did was what led me down the road that ultimately ended in the tremendous adoration and love I have for him today. Nevertheless, I will always regret having done that.

When my mother and I went to the court, there was nobody else in the room except the bailiff, the judge, and us. She and I stood at the podium, where I represented myself. I was able to speak directly to the judge. He asked me why I wanted to be legally emancipated. I told him about the opportunity to model in Japan.

"My parents can't go with me," I said, "because neither of them can leave their jobs for that length of time." I hadn't officially been given the contract yet to go to Japan, but I spoke in a way that suggested I had.

"When are you going to go back to school?" the judge wanted to know. I assured him I would be taking work with me and that I would enroll in an independent-study program when I returned, so that I could catch up on whatever I'd missed. He wanted to know where.

"Monte Vista," I said. He continued his questions, all of which I answered quickly and capably. It seemed like he wanted to make sure we had thought through every aspect and possible consequence of our request. I was careful to respond in a way that would give him no reason to think that we hadn't.

The judge gave us a thorough explanation of what legal emancipation meant. He wanted us to be mindful not only of what it would allow me to do, but also of what it would not allow me to do, such as stay on my parents' health insurance policy.

"Is this your idea?" the judge asked my mother. "Do you consent to this? Does her father consent to this?"

"Yes, sir," she said. "It's all fine. We're only doing this for work. She will still be living with me."

That was it. He granted it to me. Just like that.

I think it's hilarious how, as a little kid, when I used to run away, I'd tell my parents where they could find me. I'd take one or two things and say, "If you need me, I'll be at Ruthie's." Or "You can reach me at Madison and Gayle's." I was so sold on the idea that my parents' world revolved around me, that if I was gone, they'd eventually, for some reason, need me to come back home. Not want, *need*.

I was, I guess you could say, tethered to my parents. In a good way. There was only but so far away I could roam. Whenever I left, it was always me who wanted to get away from them. And I would do that, with the security of knowing that when I returned, nothing would have changed. Everything in the house, and everything in and between us, would be the same.

That's one thing their separation didn't change. Well, it did with my father, but only physically, because we lived on opposite coasts. Emotionally, it stayed that way with both of them. It didn't matter whether I was mad or resentful or bitter—there was only but so far those emotions could take me from who and what I was to my parents and they were to me. Through all my erratic, hormone-induced moods, I knew this. I believed then, in my heart of hearts, just as I did when I was younger, that nothing and nobody could change that.

My mom and I had been having a hard time. Some of it was my fault. I'd, at turns, been belligerent, incorrigible, and depressed to the point of being inconsolable. In short, I was an all-American teenager. Her birthday was around the corner, and I wanted to do something special for her. I wanted to give her something that she really wanted. I'd been saving my money for weeks, putting away all my paychecks, so that I could afford to buy it. When it got closer to the day, I asked her to tell me what she wanted. She became very quiet, not in a pensive way. It was more shy and hesitant.

"Nothing, honey, nothing," she finally said.

"Mom, I got a job so I can do these things. It's your first birthday here in California. We gotta celebrate somehow, you and me." She grew quiet again for a few seconds and then she said, "Could you leave the house for the weekend, for my birthday?" I didn't know what to say. I thought I hadn't heard her right.

"You want me to leave? For your birthday?" I waited for her to say something, but she didn't. "Why? Where am I supposed to go?" I asked. If I wasn't so startled, I might have started crying.

"Why do you want me to leave for your birthday?" I asked again. "Tell me." Richard came out of the other room and stood between my mother and me.

"Don't talk back to your mother like that," he said. "You heard what she said, you gotta leave the house for the weekend. That's what she wants." Well, now I was mad.

"Is that what *she* wants?" I asked him. "Or is that what *you* want? You told her to say that, didn't you, because you don't want me here." I guess I pushed him to his limit, too. A huge argument broke out between the two of us.

"Who are you?" I yelled. "You've known us for, like, seven minutes. You don't get to tell me what my mother wants." He got right up in my face, so close that he splashed me with spit when he spoke.

"You listen, young lady," he said, wagging his right pointer at me. "I'm living here. I'm helping your mother. And from now on, you're going to—"

"—I'm not going to do a damn thing," I interrupted. "You

don't get to make the rules. You're not my father." I stared at him defiantly, determined not to blink or back away from his glare. He didn't even look anything like my father. He was tall, with a big nose. His lips were thin and they became even thinner when he spoke. I leaned over and looked at my mother, wondering why she wasn't saying anything. Richard continued talking. He told me that things were going to start changing around there. I wouldn't be able to let my friends come over anymore unless either he or my mother was home. And even then, they would have to first approve the friends I had.

"Oh, please. Are you joking?" I said. Richard wasn't joking, and he wasn't done.

"You're either going to pay rent and follow those rules," he demanded, "or you're going to leave this house." It was a completely gnarly scene. I couldn't get past the shock of knowing my mom was listening to all of this and not saying a word.

"I'm not paying rent to live here. This is my mother's place. This is *our* home." I stepped aside so I could address my mother. "Hello, you're not even standing up for me here." At that, she finally spoke.

"Will you two stop it?" It was too little, too late. We weren't preschoolers fighting over the last snack-time cookie. This was some man who she had brought into our lives less than a year ago, telling me that if I didn't live according to those bogus rules he'd set up, I'd have to get out. And she was my mother— my *mother*!—standing there like a statue, letting it happen. Given a choice of who to defend, of which relationship to protect, she had chosen him. It was the ultimate betrayal. I threw my hands up.

"You know what?" I said to Richard. "Fuck you." I walked in the direction of my room. As I passed where my mother was standing, I snarled, "And you, too."

"Don't you talk to your mother that way," Richard screamed behind me.

"If I have to pay rent," I yelled into the air, as I was going to my room, "then I'm gonna live somewhere I can have my friends over and I can do whatever I want. I'm gonna live somewhere I can be happy!"

"Jaime," my mother said, "you're not going anywhere."

"Yeah, whatever," I replied, from behind the closed door. I was already packing. First, I called Chris and told him what had happened. He said he would come pick me up. Then, I called Lily and told her, too. Right away, she said, "You can come and stay here."

So I left. The tether had been broken.

I was free to go.

green

O kay, here's the thing that doesn't make sense. I'd just had the biggest blowout of my life. I'd packed everything I owned into a few bags, hopped into a car with my boyfriend, who was taking me to my best friend's house to spend the night while I figured out what to do next, and all I could think about was getting a burger and fries. Talk about being in a zone.

Everybody's threshold for pain is different, but the one thing we've all got in common is that once we endure what we can, we get to a point where we stop feeling. We become numb. Some part of the brain shuts down and says, *Enough!* I think it's the same with emotional pain. Except you don't shut down; as odd and backward as it sounds, I think you actually open up. Your heart shatters into a million little pieces, and you think it's the end of the world, but it's only the beginning, because a broken heart is essentially an open heart. All those splinters and cracks are really entrances for love.

Chris and I drove to McDonald's, where I stuffed myself. We got back into his car and headed off to Lily's. I was too mad to be scared, too hurt to be worried. I stared out the window, looking at the landscape, seeing it all but not recognizing a thing.

"You okay?" Chris asked.

"Unh-huh," I said. We drove on. He talked on and on about how messed up it all was, how a mother should never let a new man walk in and take over.

"Those guys always have their own agendas," he said. "They're master manipulators." I knew he was talking about his own mother, his own problems. I kept looking out the window. We drove. It wasn't as if we were going far. I think time had slowed down. Every minute was crawling its way forward.

"What're you thinking?" Chris wanted to know.

"I should have gotten an apple pie," I said, shrugging. I wish I could say that I was thinking of something more intense, more dramatic, but I wasn't. I'd had enough drama and intensity to last me a lifetime. What I needed now, more than anything else, was a taste of something sweet.

Evelyn and Dave Swann, Lily's mom and stepfather, made me feel welcome in their home. Lily told them what had happened, so I wouldn't have to. They gave me a place to sleep. Lily's sister, Rose, lived in Colorado with their father.

"This will be your room, Jaime," Evelyn said, opening the

door to the room that had been reserved as Rose's. I knew I wouldn't be able to fall asleep easily that night, so I stayed up with Lily. She told me that Evelyn and Dave said I could stay for as long as I needed. I was relieved to know that I didn't have to figure out what to do for the next night.

"What if I need to stay forever?" I asked Lily. I was just testing the waters. People sometimes say things they don't really mean. They'll tell you things like "you can eat as much as you want" but really what they mean is "stop at the second slice." I wanted to know if "stay as long as you want" really meant "after two weeks we'll be ready for you to move on."

"Then stay forever," Lily said nonchalantly. I heard the words but I didn't trust them. It wasn't that I didn't trust Lily, it just seemed too good to be true. How could her folks, two people who didn't know me from anywhere, take me in like that and let me stay? There had to be a catch. For the first couple of weeks, I was always on guard. I treated it like an overnight at a friend's house, which, in a way, is what it was: an extended overnight. It wasn't my home and I wasn't their child. I put myself on my best behavior and was really careful not to offend anybody by doing or saying anything wrong.

It took a lot of discipline to not let myself fall in love with Evelyn and Dave and the home they'd created, because it was everything I once had. It was the type of normal that makes for boring reading. They loved each other. They cooked together, they ate together, and they talked to each other. Evelyn and Dave were true soul mates, that couple you see at the corner diner eating off each other's plates and finishing off each other's sentences.

Evelyn was warm and fleshy. I lived for her hugs. You could just bury your face in her bosom and feel all your troubles falling away. Dave was a tall and big man, sturdy as a redwood. If you didn't know him, you might be intimidated, but once you did, his personality dwarfed his size. He liked to laugh, was always teasing but not in a pestering kind of way. He was a trickster who liked to pull pranks.

Sometimes when Lily and I would go into her room and get in her bed, Dave would be hiding down beside the frame, waiting for us to get comfortable enough so he could raise his arm up from down there and scare the living daylights out of us. We'd be on our feet, our hearts palpitating, and he'd slide out and say, "Always be aware of your environment." That was what he always said after he'd scared us half out of our wits. If it was a lesson he was trying to teach us, then I learned it well, and so did Lily. Because of him, I'm always careful coming out of a laundry room or getting into my car.

In addition to the room, Evelyn and Dave gave me rules, the same ones that Lily had to follow. They gave me an allowance and chores. They even put me on punishment with Lily when we broke the rules. They also gave me love, but I was so wounded that love wasn't enough. After the separation, after the move, the whole mess with me and Richard and my mom, it was assurance that I wanted. You can love someone and still send them away. I had to know that everything they were doing, everything they were giving was not going to be taken away from me.

One day Evelyn and Dave were talking about the future. I was watching TV, only half-listening to what they were saying. My ears perked up when I heard my name. I began paying attention. They were including me in the arrangements they were making, talking about me as if I were one of their own.

"Lily and Jaime are just going to have to . . ." I eavesdropped for a while, and then decided that their conversation was boring, just parents making plans. I went back to watching my show, but from that moment on, I knew. I knew.

The contract for Japan came through. I went in to get weighed. A hundred and eighteen pounds. It wasn't good enough for them. They wanted me to be a hundred and ten, maximum. They wouldn't let me get on that plane unless I was. I had six weeks to make it happen.

I didn't want to leave Evelyn and Dave's. I had gotten so comfortable in their home—my home—that I'd started calling Evelyn "Mom," like Lily did, with her blessings. Lily called her stepfather "Dave," so I stuck with that. I'd become a part of their family. I loved them and I'd gotten used to the quiet pace of our lives. There were no surprises. It was the same ole, same ole, and I didn't want to let that go. But I had moved to California for the dream of being a model and an actress, and I didn't want to let that go either.

From the moment I was told that I would have to lose weight, I developed a hunger that was more ravenous than anything I'd

ever known. I'd always been a big eater, but now I was more attached to food than ever. I wasn't anywhere near fat. My body
was well developed, as the editor of *Teen* magazine had told me,
but it was compact, solid muscle.

I didn't know how to begin losing weight, but I knew that I
wasn't about to give up food. I loved eating, always have. I never
realized I might have to stop eating so much in order to become
a model. No one had complained about my weight before. Exer-
cise seemed like the best way to meet my goal. I started walking more, working out. When that didn't work, I surrendered
and decided to cut down my food intake. I created an easy,
foolproof diet—two English muffins a day and water. Really it
was one English muffin, but I counted it as two, because that's
how many pieces there were after I'd split it open. Needless to
say, that diet didn't last or work. I was hungry all the time and
I wasn't losing any weight. In order to go to Japan, I absolutely
had to lose the weight, so I resorted to a practice that I felt, at the
time, was the only quick-fix solution to what I had been told was
my weight problem.

When you stick your finger down your throat, you start
to cough and then gag. Your immediate instinct is to remove
your finger and let your body recover from the violation. If you
don't, if you keep it stuck in your throat and push it down just
a little further, you start to heave. You feel the contents of your
stomach moving up toward your chest, up into your throat, and
then finally through your mouth and into the toilet or sink. The
whole thing was disgusting, but I did it because I wanted to go
to Japan.

For one week, I'd eat and then go into the bathroom afterward to purge. I looked like hell. Calluses started developing on the knuckles of the fingers I was using, my cheeks were swollen, and I smelled like vomit. I wasn't sure if anybody else noticed, but it stayed in my clothes and in the air around me. There were a few times when I suspected that Lily knew, but she didn't say anything, so I assumed that I was wrong.

One Saturday afternoon, I was hanging with Lily and her boyfriend. The three of us were having a serious chow-down. I ate everything in sight and after I was good and full, I excused myself to go to the bathroom, where I was going to force my body to throw it all up. Lily must have told her boyfriend what she thought was going on in there, because I hadn't been in that long when he knocked twice but then opened the door and walked in on me before I could say anything.

There I was, down on my knees, my chin resting on the cool, white porcelain of the toilet bowl. There were tears streaming down my cheeks. I wasn't crying. That was what always happened when I stuck my finger down my throat. I guess it was my body reflexively mourning its own destruction. I hadn't thrown up yet. I was just preparing myself for the second heave.

Lily's boyfriend picked me up off the floor. He carried me into Lily's room and threw me down on the bed, then he yelled at the top of his lungs: "You're gonna stop this shit right now!!!!!!" Lily was in the room, sitting on the floor near the bed, looking at us. She was crying, and, unlike mine, the tears were from an emotional, not a physical, reaction. I knew that what I'd been doing was wrong, and seeing Lily so upset like that made me realize it wasn't worth it. Looking back, I can't believe I ever did that. Not only was it stupid, but as a dancer and gymnast, I'd always respected my body and treated it well. I think of all the young girls who are, right now, being made to feel as I was back then, that my already slender body wasn't thin enough, wasn't perfect enough. I'd like to believe that I would have come to my senses on my own, before any real damage was done, even if I hadn't been blessed enough to have someone like Lily, who cared enough to tell me to my face that what I was doing was wrong. Thankfully, I did have Lily, and hopefully, all the models and would-be models who are considering going the route of bingeing and purging will have, if not their own conscience, the love and consideration of a friend like Lily to make them understand that it's not a road they want to begin traveling. There are other, better and safer options.

Our friend Skyla knew somebody who knew somebody who had a friend that worked as a personal trainer. With the help of Lily and Skyla, I followed the links and pleaded my way into more than a few free sessions with the trainer. He told me that the reason I wasn't losing weight was that I had almost no excess body fat. With the exception of maybe two or three pounds, any weight I dropped would be coming from the loss of lean muscle mass. He worked with me to lose those couple of pounds in a way that was healthy and safe. The next time I went to get weighed, the scale was on one hundred and fifteen. My contract for the job in Japan was confirmed. My weight was a few pounds above what they wanted, but my size and measurements were well within the range of what they required, so they went ahead and gave me my ticket.

Costa Mesa was the closest I'd ever been to a foreign country. It never crossed my mind to be frightened; I was anxious to get a break from California, a change of scenery. And that's exactly what I got. I landed in Japan and, not to be politically incorrect or anything, I felt like I had woken up in a sushi restaurant. There I was, amid all of these Japanese people—me, Jaime, blond-haired, blue-eyed me.

I didn't speak a lick of Japanese, didn't even know how to say "*konnichiwa.*" My apartment was in the Minato Ward in Tokyo, around the corner from the main drag in Roppongi. I'd never had my own apartment before, a place of my own, without adults. I had a roommate, an eighteen-year-old girl named Julie Gilmore, from Georgia. Her father was a minister or reverend, somebody who preached against the evils of everything his daughter was being exposed to in Tokyo.

Some of the models who were there, like Julie and me, were from Jonathan LaPeer's agency, but not everybody. We were all friendly with each other. Being so far away from home, we needed the companionship, but underneath all the smiles there was still the stench of competition.

I was the youngest one there, but I ended up being something of a caretaker to the others, especially my roommate, Julie, even though she was three years older than me. It's a wonder her father had even let her come to Japan. You could tell she came from a really sheltered background. She was as ignorant as the day is long, didn't know nothing about nothing. I was surprised at how naïve and vulnerable she was.

With the exception of one or two of the girls, who were old hats, it was the first time most of us had been out of the country, for work or anything else. But it wasn't as if we were living it up. All of us were perpetually broke. Compared to America, Japan was painfully expensive. A trip to McDonald's could run you into bankruptcy. We worked alright, but our sponsors kept an account for each of us. It was something of an indentured servitude. Everything we earned was applied against everything they had to put out on our behalf, like our rent and general upkeep. At the end of the day, we were lucky if we came up with one small yen coin with a hole in its center to slide around our necklaces as a keepsake. Thankfully, our employment did come with a few perks.

Most of the clubs in Roppongi would let us get in for free when we showed our professional modeling cards, which we referred to as either our comp or zed cards. A lot of the restaurants also let us eat for free. That's how many of us could afford to feed ourselves. In addition to that, Mom and Dave, my newly adopted parents, sent me care packages that contained rice, oatmeal, and other food. As glad as I was for the break and the distance, I missed everybody back home—Mom and Dave, Lily, Chris, even my parents, though I wasn't prepared to return to my mother's home or to the same broken and bitter relationships I had with her, Richard, or my father.

Roppongi was a really funky area. It bordered on being seedy. There were a lot of nightclubs, bars, and restaurants. There were a lot of foreigners, too. It was definitely multicultural. Some of the other models and I would go to the nightclubs just to stave off boredom. On our way there, we'd see Asian women—Japanese, Korean, and Chinese—wearing these long, padded coats advertising their services to every man who passed by.

"Massagee, massagee," they would yell out, while folding one hand into a fist and making rapid, jerking, up-down motions with it. The African men, in their colorful, sailor-like hats, would ask the women who passed by them, "What would you like for tonight?" I knew what they were all selling. I may have been young, but I wasn't as green as I was when I left North Carolina. If anything, I had grown hard and sharp. I was getting brown around the edges, falling from my childhood illusions, slowly and quietly, like a leaf from a tree.

When I got back, Mom and Dave took me in again. It was as if I had never left. We fell back into our pleasant but predictable routine of being a family. Lily and I continued to grow closer. She went on sharing her parents with me without ever, not even once, expressing any jealousy or making me feel like an outsider. Lily and I were so fully bonded, we referred to each other as sisters. I had been gone for two short months, but it felt like a lifetime. I'd worked a lot and earned a lot—yet, because of the way our pay had been structured, I'd only come home with five hundred dollars.

As much as I loved Lily, Mom, and Dave, being on my own in Japan for that time had unleashed something in me. I'd had my own apartment, learned to use the subway system, and stayed out all night in clubs. I had gone to a foreign country, been in the real world, and held my own. Conquering life in Costa Mesa seemed like a breeze.

While I was gone, Chris's relationship with his stepfather had taken a turn for the worse. He'd been kicked out, made to leave his house in much the same way that I'd been made to leave mine. He'd found a place to live in town and invited me to move in with him. It was a bad idea. I knew it. Lily said so, and Mom and Dave told me so when I told them that I wanted to go.

"We don't want you to do this," they said, "but we're not technically your parents." I nodded my head, but it was not in agreement. I did it only to let them know I was listening. I'd certainly come to think of them as my parents. I even felt tethered to them in the same way I'd once felt tethered to my real parents.

"You're legally emancipated," Dave reminded me. "We can't stop you from doing this, so we'll support you however you need us to. Just know that there'll always be a place for you here."

I moved out, because I was stupidly and madly in love with Chris. This time I left not because I was free to go, but because I knew I was free to come back.

men

How would a fifteen-year-old girl know what qualities to look for in a guy? Nobody had ever sat me down and taught me about men. Nobody explained to me that some of them aren't worth the time or the trouble, that no matter what you do, you can't change the way they are. There were some things I did know without anybody having to tell me. I knew that most men were regular and ordinary. They didn't raise hell or receive applause. I knew that there were a few men who were better than regular and ordinary. Those were the *good* men. I learned all this from listening to the comments women would make aloud in public.

Like one time when I was young, I saw a man, another customer, offer to help a lady carry her bags out of the Piggly Wiggly.

There were two women in line ahead of me. They looked at each other, nodded approvingly, and one of them said, "Now that's a *good* man." Another time, when we were at church, there was a young couple with a baby sitting in the pew right in front of us. The woman was holding the baby, who was irritable and fussing up a storm. Her husband said, "Here, let me take him outside for a walk." After the man had left with the baby, the woman sitting next to them touched the mother on her shoulder and said, "Honey, you got yourself a *good* man."

Naturally, considering the alternative, I wanted to one day find myself a *good* man. But if there was a secret, a method to being able to do that, the women in my family didn't pass it down. When it came to men, they didn't have many experiences to recount or mistakes they could point to and say, "Take it from me, Jaime, don't fall for that the way I did."

Aunt Careen got married at the age of seventeen. That was too old to make her a child bride, but it also didn't leave her much time to sow any wild oats. Thankfully, the man she settled down with just so happened to be a *good* man. The same goes for my mom. She hooked up with my dad when she was eighteen. He was her first and only, until they got divorced. But even then, it wasn't like she did a whole lot of dating. The next man in her life lived only five feet away.

The only other woman who could've given me useful advice was Grandmamma Pressly, who'd been with Granddaddy since the beginning of time. Nevertheless, I'm sure she probably did believe that she shared a few words of wisdom with me on the topic of men. The problem is, I couldn't understand half of what she said, and the other half was so uncomplimentary it'd make you want to become a spinster.

She once told me that "a whistling woman and a crowing hen never come to a good end." Good luck deciphering that one at twelve years old. On several other occasions, Grandmamma told me, "All men cheat. Find me a man that doesn't cheat and I'll give you a dime."

When I started dating, the limited amount I knew about men came from being around them. My family is mostly made up of men, and each one brought into my consciousness an appreciation of a specific trait or virtue, the thing that made him *good*.

With my granddaddy, it was compassion. Granddaddy Pressly had a gift for determining which part of your spirit was the most parched, and he would find a way to shower it with his love. When my cousins and I stayed at our grandparents' house, I would always end up in trouble with Grandmamma. Nothing I did pleased her, and that made me feel incredibly insecure, especially since everything my cousins did seemed to go over well.

Granddaddy would always come find me and take me with him to his study, which was just off to the side of his bedroom. We would go in there and he would lock the door so the other kids couldn't come in. There was a great big piano in there. We'd sit at the piano and I would listen to him play, watching those long fingers of his move quickly across the keyboard. He'd pick a few songs, simple tunes, and he'd teach me how to play them. I would fumble through them and Granddaddy would compliment me each note of the way, regardless of how badly I screwed up. With him, in that room, I could do no wrong. It was our special time, and for that hour or so, I was his favorite.

My dad must have inherited that part of his personality from Granddaddy. Out of all his brothers, he's regarded as the softest, a big ole softie. He takes everything to heart and has no shame about shedding tears. Dad would cry at my dance recitals. He would cry when he saw me dressed up for any landmark event—my first Christmas pageant, my first party, my first time cheerleading.

There's a famous McDonald's commercial that used to run every holiday season. It shows a group of kids—dressed in thick coats, knitted hats, and scarves—ice skating with Ronald McDonald in a winter wonderland, complete with an animated owl, deer, and rabbits. They all hold hands in a line, with Ronald McDonald in the lead, and then they skate away. The youngest of the bunch, who is on the end, lets go of the hand he is holding, loses his balance, and falls flat on his butt. He starts weeping as the others skate away. From out of nowhere, Ronald McDonald comes back, picks the boy up, and holds him in the air while skating around in a circle. Ronald McDonald smiles at him lovingly. The boy's eyes light up and he smiles, too.

It's a cheesy little commercial, but it fits in well with the general peace-and-love-to-all-mankind theme that's marketed during those December weeks. Whenever my dad used to see that commercial, he'd lose it. He'd weep right along with the little boy, and continue crying even after the boy had stopped.

My father might be the most emotionally demonstrative, but sensitivity is a shared attribute of the Pressly men. It comes out in different ways, though. In my uncle Ezra, it came out as grace. The man faced every battle he ever fought, including the one he ultimately lost his life to, with such dignity.

The uncle who I spent the most time with was my cousins Madison and Gayle's dad, Pruitt. I was always at their house, and not only because I was close with his kids. I loved being at Uncle Pruitt's because he kept a beautiful home. He is the quintessential metrosexual, the male answer to Martha Stewart.

Uncle Pruitt is the most stylish, tasteful, and creative person I've ever known. Whether it's with clothing or furniture, he can mix and match colors, fabrics, designs. He's got a keen eye, and an emerald-green thumb. His garden is a wonder to behold. Half of Kinston drives by his house to admire his azalea bushes when they're in bloom. And he's second to none in the kitchen. Uncle Pruitt's homemade pimento cheese is so amazing you'll be dreaming of it in your sleep for days afterward.

The jewel in Uncle Pruitt's crown is his originality. If anybody needed a slogan, a title, or a unique catchphrase, they'd ask Uncle Pruitt. He came up with the name of my mom's dance school, Studio 86. There was this guy, a friend of the family, whose name was Mr. Schidte. The way the story was told is that Mr. Schidte had a necktie business that wasn't doing too well. Uncle Pruitt suggested that he revamp the company and change the name of the line to "Another Shitty Necktie." He did, and it was a huge success.

There's a Southern saying that goes, "the quickest way to double your money is to fold it up and put it back in your pocket."

If I didn't know any better, I'd say that my Uncle Zane came up with it. He's the money man in our family, was the president of a bank for most of his professional years. The joke about Uncle Zane is that if there's a family dinner and everybody's supposed to pay fifty bucks apiece, he'll only bring a twenty, pull it out, and say, "That's all I've got." He's smart about how he spends—and saves—his money.

Despite his white-collar, corner-office life, Uncle Zane is a through-and-through artist, who can paint and draw the pants off of anybody. His specialty is carving. He'll take a big block of wood and carve out the most beautiful figures of mallard ducks, egrets, seagulls, any kind of bird that takes to the water.

Another man who greatly influenced me was Chuck Hathaway, Ruthie's dad. We weren't related, but we might as well have been, seeing as how I spent so much time around that family. Mr. Hathaway never said much, and he wasn't an especially affectionate person. The thing about him that made an impact on me was his work ethic and his focus.

He started out making biscuits at the local Bojangles, because he wanted to learn the business from the ground up. I'd never seen anybody work as hard as he did. His drive was almost unreal. His plan was to own that Bojangles and now he does, along with over four hundred others—and most of the town of Kinston.

I had the privilege of spending time with all of these men, these *good* men. And they were, in combination, my ideal man. So how did I end up moving in with somebody like Chris Zucker, who wasn't just in a gang but was the head of a gang? You could look at him—his shaved head, scornful eyes, and swagger—and tell that he was trouble.

Chris wasn't my first boyfriend. I started dating—*really* dating—during my freshman year at Kinston High. I went out with three different guys that year—Jake, Casey, and Brad.

Jake was a short guy. He was cordial and clever, with a good sense of humor, but he had a classic little-man complex. If he couldn't have you completely, he didn't want you at all, and I wasn't about to let myself be counted as one of his conquests. He broke up with me to date one of the other cheerleaders, a girl who would give him what he wanted to make him feel like an emperor.

Casey was a junior. He raced barrel horses and won a world championship while we were still in school. He lived out in the country with tons of land on the property and lots of horses. I'd never felt as comfortable with a guy as I did with him. He took me to his prom, and had I not been so set on leaving North Carolina, he and I might have stayed together. I wanted to squeeze in as much as I could before I left, because I didn't know what was in store for me out there in California, so I ended things between Casey and me and started dating Brad, who was a senior.

Brad and I weren't really together long enough for me to get to know him well one way or the other. Being with him was like getting a plate of food five minutes before closing time at a restaurant. You only take in enough to satisfy the hunger, and you're so preoccupied with hurrying up and getting out that you forget to let yourself taste the flavor of what you're chewing.

All three of those guys were clean-cut and likable, as was Blaise, the guy I dated when I first got to Costa Mesa High. He was a jock and an honor-roll student, whose parents preferred that he devote more time to studying than to dating me. We lasted all of one or two months. And after him came Chris.

The problems that both Chris and I had with our parents made us feel that we had much more in common than we actually did. Love can make you see in somebody what they don't even see in themselves. When Chris was around me, he became a *good* man. He became compassionate and sensitive. The rest of it, how he was when he wasn't around me, I thought I could fix. Maybe that's why it was so easy to fall in love with him. Everything else that was bad or wrong in my life couldn't be fixed, not by me, except Chris. He was well on his way down a path that was going to take him either to prison or to his grave. I thought that with time I could save him from those two options. I would soon come to find out that sometimes the thing you're trying to change ends up changing you. And that time is not the only thing which separates the boys from the men—namely the bad boys from the *good* men.

relay

The apartment that Chris and I moved into was a two-bedroom, which would have been more than enough room for us if we hadn't had so many roommates. Larry, his sister Samantha, who we called Sam, and their mother, Mildred, also lived in the apartment. Mildred slept on the couch in the living room, Larry and Sam shared one bedroom, and Chris and I shared the other.

Larry used to be the number one basketball player at Costa Mesa High, but he decided that he didn't want to do that anymore, so he stopped. Instead, he got involved with gangs, then, after that, started dabbling in drugs. Everybody in that apartment, besides Chris and me, had at one time gone astray and was now trying to get their lives back in order. Chris didn't start getting into his more questionable activities until after our relationship ended, though I highly doubt one had anything to do with the other.

Sam used to be a Goth girl, one of those chicks you see who're all done up in black from head to toe and look like extras from the set of *Night of the Living Dead* or some other zombie flick. Back then, when she was into that scene, she had a shaved head and she experimented with a lot of drugs. When I met her, she was twenty-three, sober, and dressed like your average person on the street. The only remnants of her riotous days were the tattoos, which covered nearly three-quarters of her body.

Mildred, their mother, had raised Larry and Sam on her own, because their dad was a no-show. She was also clean and sober, but all that hard living and struggling still showed on her face.

It was a large number of people to try to pack into a small number of square feet, but we managed. Part of what made it doable was that all of us worked so damned much. I was going to school full-time and working at Surf Break, a small café in the back of a surf shop. All day long I made sandwiches and smoothies for the customers. It was depressing.

Even though we lived with Mildred, she was more friend than authority figure. There were no rules. She basically let us do whatever we wanted, which probably was as it should have been, because we were pulling our own weight around the place. Everybody bought their own food and paid for their part of the rent and utilities.

Considering that there were so many of us running in and out of that place, we did well to keep it as clean and orderly as we did. Because the living room also served as Mildred's bedroom, we didn't leave a whole lot of junk lying around. As unconventional as they may have been, Larry, Sam, and Mildred were a family. And since Chris and I were together as a couple, the two of us were also something of a family. So what probably seemed, from the outside looking in, like five wayward people roughing it in a run-down apartment, was actually two families with limited resources coming together and sharing a home.

My brother, Junior, is nine and a half years older than me. When I was little, he was my idol. I used to look up to him so much. I used to even try to be him. I'd talk the way he did, dress the way he did. Whatever shoes he was wearing, you'd better believe I tried my best to fill.

In our family, history tends to repeat itself. I used to think of Junior often. I'd try to remember how he was when he was fifteen and sixteen years old, because it gave me hope that it was more than likely I'd turn out all right. Junior was tall, with dirty-blond hair, bright green eyes, and those full Pressly lips. He got all of that from our side of the family. From his mother, Verna Nell, he got his dark olive complexion and, I'm sure, many other less immediately discernible but equally admirable traits.

Junior used to play baseball when he was growing up. When he was a senior in high school, he had scholarship offers coming at him from left and right. But his girlfriend got pregnant, and he dropped out of school two months before graduation. He married her—the same way our dad had married Junior's mother when she'd gotten pregnant in high school. They had a little girl, Stacey, my niece. Junior's marriage to Stacey's mom lasted three years, which is exactly how long our dad's marriage to Verna Nell lasted, and then they got divorced.

After the divorce, Junior left Kinston to piece together a future for himself somewhere else. He went as far south as Florida and then slowly started inching his way back to our hometown. He lived in Greenville, and then Raleigh, and then, finally, he settled down in Kinston.

I wondered if that would be the way things would work out for me, if I would find myself leaving California and heading east, going from city to city, each one a little bit closer to Kinston, and then, finally, come to terms with the idea of returning to my roots.

Every day, when I was making those sandwiches, slathering mayonnaise on top of those pieces of bread and slapping that turkey or bologna or ham in between, I'd think about my big brother. I'd replay a lot of the things he told me when I was little, things I never suspected would one day be useful to me.

Tagging was becoming really big in Orange County, especially with gang members. Many nights, Chris would go to meet his buddies on the street so they could graffiti the side of a building, or a bridge, or a freeway overpass with their symbols and cryptic messages. All the guys would leave their girlfriends at home, where we would wait for them, frightened that they might get busted while doing their deed. Girls weren't allowed in their gang yet, not that I would have joined had they let me.

The gangs, many of which had really been nothing more

than a club of tough-guy-wannabes who talked a good game, were growing and becoming more active in crime and violence. There was the usual defacing of public property, but then theft and other illegal albeit petty activities also became a more prominent part of their reason for being.

I'd gotten used to the presence of gangs and gang-bangers. I was still friendly with a lot of the Latino gang members I used to talk to when I first started going to Costa Mesa High. I didn't see it as *my* world, because I didn't take part in it. But it was *a* world that I witnessed on a daily basis and floated in and out of, because Chris took part in it.

After we'd been living in the apartment for several months, the five of us decided to move into a larger place. I'd taken an additional job, doing retail at a local clothing store, and the rest of our household was also able to afford the additional rent, so we rented a house a few blocks away from the high school.

Mildred, Sam, and I were the ones who'd found the house, and, boy, were we proud of ourselves. It was a three-bedroom, with a huge living room, spacious kitchen, a den, a sizable backyard, and a garage. It was progress, a step forward in the direction of prosperity.

After we'd signed the lease, we took ourselves to lunch. All of us agreed that a much bigger celebration was in order. On Halloween night, there was going to be a football game at the high school. It was the perfect occasion for a party. We invited everyone to come back to our house after the game. If our team won, that would give us one more reason to celebrate.

That day, before the game, Mildred, Sam, and I went out and

bought food and drinks. We went the extra mile and bought decorations to spice up the atmosphere. We spent the rest of the afternoon cleaning up the house, hanging and taping stuff up, and screwing in the orange lightbulbs we'd bought to temporarily replace the regular clear ones.

A couple of people showed up early, while the football game was still going on. We were all hanging out talking when a fight broke out between two of the girls. They were on the ground, wrestling each other. Both of them were wearing Starter-style jackets. One of them, Tonia, who was on the bottom, was wearing a Raiders jacket, which was silver-and-black. The other girl, Betty, who was on top of Tonia, had on a Bulls jacket, which was red-and-black.

Betty looked like she was pounding Tonia to a pulp. Her fists were moving so fast all you could see was a blur of skin. Tonia's movements were forceful, but slow and a little stiff. I was afraid Betty was going to cause Tonia some serious damage. I turned to Chris, Larry, and the other guys who were standing with them.

"You all have to stop this," I insisted. I knew that nobody wanted to be the one to try. When you put yourself in the middle of a fight like that, instead of stopping it, you usually find yourself being pulled into it, having to throw a few punches of your own just to protect yourself.

Isaac, one of Larry's friends, moved up and stood closer to where the girls were. "If you're gonna fight, then you have to hit her," he told Tonia. "Hit her back, or else do something to get her off you." Tonia turned her head and looked at him.

"I'm fucking stabbing her," she told him. "I'm stabbing

her." Unbeknownst to us, Tonia had a pocketknife with her. The handle was hidden in her hand, so none of us could see it. During those deliberate, jerky movements she'd been making, she'd been thrusting the knife's three-inch blade into Betty's back. As soon as we heard what Tonia said, the boys all jumped in at once and pulled the girls apart. It'd been hard to see, while Betty was on the ground in her red-and-black jacket, that there was blood everywhere, but once they pulled her up, it was obvious that she'd been hurt real bad.

Mildred, who'd been in another part of the house, came out as the boys were holding Betty up.

"Oh my God," she screamed. She was hysterical. We were all freaking out, wondering what to do. "She's gotta go to the hospital," Mildred screamed. "Somebody's gotta take her to the hospital right NOW!"

The guys carried Betty to Isaac's van. We all piled in and drove to the hospital, where we found out she'd been stabbed eleven times, mostly in the spine. The damage was extensive, including a punctured lung, but Betty lived.

There's a reason why I'd always emulated my brother, a reason why my mind would wander to him as I'd pour the bowls of sliced fruits into the blender to make those smoothies. Junior told me once that he'd made a promise to me when I was born.

"That promise," he said, "was what made me keep going whenever I wanted to stop and throw in the towel." I was born a few months before his tenth birthday. Of course, Junior knew that my mom was pregnant with me, but trucks and sneakers and catchers' mitts are the things that impress nine-year-old boys, not babies. He couldn't have cared the least about having a little sister.

When he saw me for the first time, he experienced something that he couldn't explain. Every fiber of his being was touched by that feeling. My mom placed me in his arms, and he nervously cradled me.

"I was so scared I was gonna drop you." He laughed. "You were so tiny." While he was holding me, I looked up at him. He held a finger out near my hand; I grabbed it and held on tightly. He leaned his head down and spoke to me softly so nobody else could hear what he was saying. It was then that he made the promise.

"From the moment I held you," he shared with me, "I knew you were mine, and I knew I had to do whatever it took to make you proud of me. I told you, 'I promise to always try to give you a reason to keep looking up to me. I promise to always take care of you and protect you.'"

Junior was a black sheep. There were a few in our family. I think anyone who didn't fit into Grandmamma Pressly's vision of what they should be was considered a black sheep. And that was definitely Junior. He is one of those people who go left when everybody thinks they should be going right, and sometimes it turns out that everybody was correct after all, going right might very well have made the journey easier—but it wouldn't have made it his.

When Junior told me about the promise, I thought it was one of the most beautiful things I'd ever heard. Until then, the way

I'd defined the roles in our relationship was with him as the leader and me as the follower. I was his shadow.

"Shadow?" He laughed. "No, Jaime, more like my light."

My mother called. It'd been seven or eight months since I'd spoken with her, and that last time it wasn't exactly a conversation, more an exchange of information.

"Jaime?" she said through the receiver. She was calling to tell me something. I could hear it in her voice. Something important. I knew it wasn't anything bad. If it had been, she would have sounded different.

"You're pregnant, aren't you?" I asked. I imagined her facial expression, the surprise that was in those wide eyes of hers when she heard me guess correctly.

"Yes, I am. How did you—"

"That's great," I told her. It was great. I was glad for her. She'd agreed to leave North Carolina and come to California with me because she wanted to start a new life, and now she was, literally. I wasn't sure where I fit into this new life, being that I wasn't even a part of the old one anymore. She invited me to come spend Christmas with her and Richard. I was hesitant at first, unsure that I wanted to see Richard or be around him. But I did want to see my mother and spend time with her, so I went, and it was nice.

We stayed in communication throughout the rest of her pregnancy, but it wasn't constant and nothing had really changed. It wasn't as if I was going to be moving back in with them anytime soon.

Not long after the stabbing incident, Chris and I moved out of that house. We were now living in another house, with some other kids and their mom. This time, despite her assertions, I'm not so sure the mom was completely clean and sober. I suspected, at the very least, she was still secretly hitting the bottle, which meant our house was a way station for a cast of interesting, if not totally desirable, characters.

On March 29, I got a call from Richard. The baby had been born. It was a girl. Ordinarily, Chris would have given me a ride to the hospital, but he was in jail. It was starting to feel like a regular occurrence. He'd been locked up a few times already. They were all minor offenses, but jail is still jail.

I took a cab to the hospital. My mom was still in surgery, so I waited in her room with Richard. The tension in there was as heavy as a boulder. He was antsy. He kept getting up and leaving the room to go stare through the glass at his new daughter. When he came back into the room, he'd look at me. I could tell that he was searching for something to say, but there wasn't anything to be said.

They wheeled my mom in, and she got into the bed. I was sitting in a chair, really distant, but looking straight at her and talking with her. Then the nurse brought the baby in and put her in the clear hospital crib that was by my mother's bed. My little sister, Becky. She looked exactly like the Gerber baby. As soon as the nurse left, I walked over to the crib and scooped her up. That's what living in an animal house will do to you. You forget your manners. You act without thinking. I had become so unpolished—in my behavior, in my attitude, and in my carriage. I looked grubby and unkempt. I looked like what I was, a kid who nobody was taking care of.

"Hey. What the hell are you doing?" Richard asked. "Your mother's gotta hold the baby first. She was in surgery and she hasn't held the baby yet. You don't hold the baby before your mother does. It's her baby." My mother sat up a bit in the bed.

"Would you just stop?" she told him. "Let her hold the baby. We're gonna be holding her for the rest of our lives." It was the first time my mother had stood up for me with Richard, the first time she'd chosen to take my side over his. My eyes were welling up. I looked over at my mother.

"Go ahead," she said. I held Becky in my arms, walked over to the chair, and sat down. I remembered what Junior had said to me about the first time he'd held me. Becky looked up at me. I wanted to do for her what Junior had done for me. I wanted to be somebody she could look up to, someone whose footsteps were worth following. I let Becky wrap her little hand around my pinkie.

How did this happen? I wondered. I was seventeen years old and my life was a disaster. How did it get this far? I didn't grow up this way. I wasn't raised this way. My childhood was solid, as solid as they come, in a small town with trees and nice houses and people who loved me. I'd never committed a crime, barely drank, and didn't use drugs. I'd always been ambitious, a go-getter, the sort of person who was not only focused but fearless about pursuing her goals. Why was I living in a house with people who, try as they did to pull themselves together, were teetering on the edge of some sort of self-destruction, and dating the leader of a gang who was in and out of jail?

Tears started pouring down my face. I couldn't let Becky go. I held my head down so my mother and Richard wouldn't see that I was crying. And I said to my little sister—in my head, so that they wouldn't hear me, "I promise you I'm gonna get better. I'm gonna give you a reason to look up to me. I'm gonna get better. I swear."

"Jaime," my mom said softly, "whenever you're ready." I got up with Becky, walked over to Richard, and gave her to him.

Richard was a mama's boy. Everybody in his family says so. His mother is said to have been a dynamic woman, and the two of them had always been incredibly close. About a month and a half before Becky was born, Richard's mom found out that she had a brain tumor. A few days later, she was dead.

When Richard took Becky from me, he held her up, high in the air, with his arms fully outstretched. He looked up at her, looked past her at the ceiling, and if he could have, he would have probably looked past that into the heavens. He said, "Mama, look what I did. Look what I did." He brought Becky down and held her to his heart, and he started bawling. My mother started crying, too. I had never stopped, but seeing Richard like that with Becky made my tears flow faster and harder.

Richard's love for Becky was profound. Now he knew what it was to have a child, to have that sort of bond. He would never do to Becky what he had done to me. He would never make her leave his home. I'd like to believe that he realized what he had done to my mother and me. Even if that's not the case, I realized right then and there that he hadn't known any better.

From that day on, I saw Richard in a different light. I saw life in a different light. It was the first time that we were like a family. In that room, everything changed, for each of us. Babies will do that.

language

Sometimes you find that what looks to be a curse is actually a bona fide blessing. My third-grade teacher Miss Culpepper taught me that, but not on purpose. She was a mean, weasel-faced woman who didn't have enough patience to deal with small children. She'd have probably been better suited for a different job—something like, oh, a factory foreperson—because she was so good at barking out orders and being intimidating.

I used to think back to Miss Culpepper's class from time to time, when I first started acting. I'd be holding a script in my hand, saying my lines out loud, and I'd remember how that ole battle-ax used to hover over me whenever it was my turn to read out loud in class.

"We're waiting, Jaime," she'd say. "What's taking you so long?" Reading words in your head and reading them aloud are two completely different skills. Like most kids my age, I learned how to read by sight. "Whole language" is what they call that method. It's when a kid learns to read by memorizing an entire word and its meaning. When I saw a word, I didn't just know what it was and what it meant, I could even hear it being sounded out in my head. But making it come out of my mouth was a whole 'nother story. I had to break the word down phonetically, let the sound of each letter slide from my brain to my tongue before I could spit it out, so it'd usually take me a minute or two to get myself in order. And that was a minute or two longer than Miss Culpepper wanted to wait.

"Is there a problem, Jaime?"

I'd shake my head and then I'd begin, even though I wasn't really ready.

"The c-c-c-ca-a—"

"Cat," she'd snap, before I had a chance to finish. "The word is 'cat.' Now go on to the next one."

My hands would start shaking, which would make the book unsteady, which made everything worse, because then all the letters would move around like squiggly little insects. I'd take a deep breath and continue.

"L-l-liked the b—"

"That's not the right word, Jaime," Miss Culpepper would cut me off in a huff. "It's 'licked,' not 'liked.' Didn't you see the c before the k? Pay attention! Now pick up where you left off!"

That's how it was whenever we read out loud or practiced

spelling, which was also a major part of Miss Culpepper's class. She always turned me into a spectacle, made me feel like a dunce, like I should be sitting in some high chair in the corner of the room with a huge hat on my head. I was scared to death of making a mistake. It got so bad that sometimes when she called on me, I'd start to hyperventilate, but that didn't matter to her; she'd still force me to read or spell.

So how'd I get from there to here, from being scared to death of reading out loud to confidently delivering lines from scripts I've never even seen before in front of casting directors and producers? My dad, that's how. Leave it to a Pressly to find a way to take the most frightening activity in somebody's life and turn it into fodder for a performance.

The evening-time was when my mother's dance studio would be in full swing. That's because the bulk of her students were in school during the day. Since my father was the one at home, more often than not he was the one who helped me with my homework. Miss Culpepper had everybody believing I probably had a learning disability that had me bordering on being functionally illiterate, so my forever-optimistic father went overboard to help me overcome it.

Dad would pull out the baton I used when I was a majorette. He'd have me stand behind him and follow his moves while he marched around the house like we were in front of a band, leading the way. He'd make each word on my spelling list a cheer and repeat it over and over and over again until it was drilled into my memory. Every Friday, Miss Culpepper quizzed us on our spelling, so on Thursday nights, Dad and I would march until the soles of our feet were pounding with pain.

"C'mon, Chicken," he'd say, calling me by my pet name. "Because. B-e-c-a-u-s-e. B-e-c-a-u-s-e. B-e-c-a-u-s-e. Because? Because! B-e-c-a-u-s-e. B-e-c-a- . . ." Dad would be so into it, you'd think he was the one who was practicing for a good grade. He'd hold the baton out, then up, then twirl it around his head. He'd lift his knees high. Left then right then left again. I'd do the same, focusing as much on keeping up my pace as on repeating the cheer. "B-e-c-a-u-s-e. B-e-c-a-u-s-e."

In addition to learning how to spell the words, I'd have to write a story using all of the words on the list for that week. After we'd marched around the house a gazillion times, spelling out each word, Dad would put the baton down and go sit at the table.

"You can do it, Chicken," he'd say, urging me to think up sentences using the words on my list. "I know you can. Just let your imagination go." He and I would come up with the craziest stories. We'd have so much fun—too much fun—and the miracle would start to happen: I'd fall in love again with language. I'd remember that words were these great vehicles that could take me anywhere, drive me deep into any fantasy. And I would let myself be swept away . . . until it was time for me to read in front of Miss Culpepper.

My parents also placed me with a tutor, Miss Hart, to work with me on my reading and spelling. Her plan was for us to start from scratch and work our way up into an entire vocabulary.

"A-e-i-o-u. Those are the vowels of the English language." It was our first session. I was to repeat after her. The plan was that we would study one vowel during each of our sessions, and Miss Hart would teach me the different ways you could sound them out in words.

"Let's start with *a*. Ah. Do you know a word that begins with *a*?"

"Arachnophobia," I said. You should have seen Miss Hart's eyes pop right out of her head. I guess she was expecting a simpler word, seeing as how she'd been told I was a kid who could barely read the word "cat" out loud from a book.

"Arachnophobia? Now that's an interesting word to choose. But do you know what it means?" She probably thought I was trying to smart off and she was trying to gently put me back in my place, but the problem was that I was never supposed to be in that place to begin with. I didn't have any learning disabilities. I knew how to read and how to spell just as well as anybody else in my class, probably better.

"That's when you're afraid of spiders," I told her. Since that didn't work, she tried another angle.

"Can you spell it?" I'd learned that word because I'd been reading the dictionary. I'd been made to feel like such a moron in Miss Culpepper's class because I'd screwed up trying to read such small words. I'd known all of those words and I wouldn't have had a problem saying them if it hadn't been for all that pressure Miss Culpepper put on me. I'd wanted to prove that I wasn't as dumb and delayed as everybody was starting to think I was, so I'd started learning and memorizing difficult words from the dictionary. I spelled it for her, slowly but correctly.

"Where'd you learn that?" Miss Hart wanted to know. I shrugged. She looked at me suspiciously for a second and then she reached into her bag and grabbed a book. She opened it to a random page, pointed to the first line at the top, and said, "Read that." I took my time and read it aloud, word for word. My hands didn't shake and I didn't read one word incorrectly. Miss Hart got out another book, opened that, pointed to a line, and said, "Read this." I read that one, too. We went through about five books. The first one was the easiest. The others got harder and harder as she went along. She finally gave me one with words I'd never seen before and couldn't really read very well, but by then she'd also figured out that my problem with reading and spelling didn't have anything to do with what was on the page. It had everything to do with my fear of Miss Culpepper.

"Jaime's far above the third-grade reading level," Miss Hart reported to my parents. They were relieved to hear the news, but it didn't come as much of a surprise to them, especially my father, who had already gotten a glimpse of my full potential.

By the time I met Miss Henrietta Mills, I knew how to prove people wrong. I'd done it more than a few times. Truth be told, having somebody tell you what you're not capable of doing can sometimes even be a little inspiring. It's like a challenge—and I was always up for a good challenge. I knew what I was good for, so rolling up my sleeves and saying "Oh yeah? Watch this" was a whole lot more than a notion.

Miss Mills came into my life well before my sister, Becky, was born. She taught me English in the independent-studies program I was doing. That was the one subject I was really good at, and I got along with Miss Mills, so I kept enrolling in her class. One of the assignments Miss Mills would give me was to write stories. We were working on grammar and punctuation, and that was her way of seeing how well I had grasped and could apply what she had taught me. When I first started writing for Miss Mills, the stories that I handed in were all made up, pure fiction. Writing them reminded me of those Thursday-night sessions with my dad, how we used to turn my homework into a family project.

Changing my life had in itself become something of a project, and the first phase of it was a return to the foundation of family. In an effort to keep the promise I'd made to Becky that day in the hospital, I moved out of the group house where I'd been living with Chris. I phoned Mom and Dave and asked them if I could live with them again. They said yes.

That ole adage about love dying hard is so true. I still loved Chris and I still felt that I could save him from the world and from himself, but living with Mom and Dave gave me fewer and fewer opportunities to do so. If there was one person who Dave Swann just wasn't having, it was Chris Zucker. Dave didn't want him anywhere near his home or me. I didn't want to defy Dave, who was the closest thing west of the Mississippi I had to a father, but I also didn't want to deny what I felt for Chris.

Things just seemed like such a mess. There was a lot to think about, so many things to figure out. So I wrote about it all. Instead of the usual fantastical creations that I handed in, one week I gave Miss Mills a true-to-life account of what I was going through. I hadn't intended to write about myself. It's just what came out when I sat down and started scribbling.

I wrote about love, about Chris and me, about how sometimes love puts you in a position of having to choose between it and everything else in your life. I wrote about how painful it is to try to make that decision, how frightening it is to not know whether you're making the right choice.

There were a few grammatical errors, misspellings, and some misplaced punctuation, but other than that, Miss Mills loved the story. She said it was the best piece of writing she'd ever read from me, and she encouraged me to do the same thing with my next assignment, to write a story from my life.

So I did. Every week, I'd hand in a new story. I wrote about Kinston and my family there; I wrote about my parents and their new spouses; I wrote about all the moving I had done and about where I'd been and what I'd seen. But mostly, I wrote about how disappointed I was that so few of the dreams I'd had when I left Kinston had come true.

Every week Miss Mills would read my story and she would cry. She'd correct my mistakes and then she'd tell me how much the story had touched her, how she could really relate to it. I thought it was something she was just saying to be nice, but then one day she shared her own story with me. After hearing that, I could see that she was being honest with me about my work.

Like me, Miss Mills had wanted to be an actress. She'd gone to school and studied to perfect her craft. She'd even had a couple of small parts here and there. The only other thing that mattered to her besides her career was her boyfriend. The two of them were in love and had big plans for their future together. Miss Mills auditioned for a part in a Broadway play and she was cast as the lead, starring opposite Gene Hackman. It was a huge break, and Miss Mills was out of her mind with excitement. It was exactly the kind of opportunity she needed to get her career off the ground. Unfortunately, her boyfriend wasn't as thrilled with the idea of her going to New York to work. He couldn't go with her, and he didn't want to be left behind. He made it clear to her that if she went, it would mean the end of their relationship. So Miss Mills had a choice to make: the love of a man or the love of her dream. Well, at the time, being with that man was also a dream, so she chose him.

I never asked Miss Mills what became of the man. I didn't have to. I could tell from the way she spoke of him that even if he was still in her life, she'd realized that she'd made the wrong choice. She'd walked away from the dream that, in the long run, truly mattered most.

"Jaime, you can still do this," Miss Mills would tell me. "Nothing has passed you by yet."

"I dunno," I'd say to her. I wasn't even eighteen and I felt old and defeated. "I dunno if I can."

"Yes," Miss Mills would insist. "You can." She said it in the same way and with the same tone that people had said "You *can't*" to me. And after a while, I got that it was the same sort of challenge. Except instead of wanting me to prove her wrong, what Miss Mills was daring me to do was prove her right.

———

The drive from Costa Mesa to Los Angeles takes about an hour, if there's no traffic—and anybody who knows Southern California knows that there's always traffic. It was complicated to get around Costa Mesa and its surrounding areas without a car. The transit system was skeletal at best, catering only to the bare necessities of its residents. Trying to use public transportation to go beyond the city limits was a joke, a near-impossible feat.

Hearing Miss Mills's story, especially on the heels of making the promise that I'd made to Becky, recharged my drive. She was right; it wasn't too late. And even if it was, I still had to try—for my sister's sake, if not my own. The only thing standing between me and Los Angeles, where all of the legitimate acting work was taking place, was a car.

As it turns out, I had the perfect solution to that problem. After my dad stopped working at Pressly's Laundry, he became a car salesman. It was a profession that suited him and his talents perfectly. He was good with people. He was the type of person that people felt they could trust. J. L. Pressly wasn't anything at all like the stereotypical slick, smarmy, tell-them-what-they-want-to-hear car salesman. He valued the trust that his customers placed in him, and worked hard to maintain it. Because of that, his sales figures were consistently high and he maintained a steady roster of return customers and referrals.

I certainly couldn't afford to buy a car on my own, so I decided to call my dad and ask him to get me one. It took a bit of whining and cajoling, but he agreed to help me out. The catch was that I'd have to get the car from North Carolina to California myself.

Chris was out of jail, and even though we hadn't been seeing much of each other, we were still very much involved and committed. I asked him if he would go with me to North Carolina to pick up the car and drive cross-country to Costa Mesa. He agreed, so I was set.

Grandmamma Pressly, of all people, just adored Chris. I'm sure his buzz cut had something to do with it, since she'd favored that low-maintenance hairstyle for all of her sons while they were growing up. In her book, a shaved head on a young man was a good sign. Or it could have just been that Chris was so quiet and self-contained. I don't think he said more than ten words the entire week we were in Kinston. The poor guy was far out of his element. It wasn't just being in North Carolina; it was being around the whole Pressly family. It must have all been overwhelming for him.

Chris had met me against the backdrop of newness and turmoil in a place where I didn't have anything to call my own. I was embroiled in a battle against myself and the world. That was a context he could understand. In North Carolina, I was engaged with my family, entrenched in all the vestiges of my past life. He must have had a hard time reconciling the Jaime he knew, the one who had lived with him in all those substandard housing situations, followed him into the lifestyle of the fallen and the broken, with the Jaime that sat in Grandmamma Pressly's house with the large porch, white gazebo, and fig trees in the yard. I know I did.

"Why don't you marry him?" Grandmamma asked me.

"Um, because I'm only seventeen," I reminded her.

"That's not too young. Your aunt, Careen, got married at seventeen." I stared at my grandmother blankly, like she was an alien who'd just dropped down from Mars. I said the first thing that came to mind, something that, in my mind, would easily defend my position.

"He cheats. I'm not gonna marry somebody who cheats."

"Oh," Grandmamma Pressly sneered. I knew exactly what she was gonna say next. I didn't even have to stay and listen. I'd heard it too many times. "Like I say, find me a man who doesn't cheat and I'll give you a dime."

"Only a dime, Grandmamma?" I asked. With every other challenge she posed, she'd offer a quarter, but when it had something to do with men, she always changed up to a dime.

"Let me tell you something. You're lucky to get even that for just one, 'cause usually they're only worth a dime for a dozen."

The car Dad got me was a used Honda Accord, but I knew it would bring me good luck, because of its color. It was Carolina blue, just like that sky I used to stare into when I was little. I knew that this was the car that would drive me straight into my dreams. Miss Mills was right; I could still make them come true. I would.

After our visit with my family, Chris and I got into my "new" car and drove away. It was a familiar scene, the two of us in a car, driving me into an unknown future, except this time, I was behind the wheel. We drove from North Carolina into Tennessee, the home of the other Presley family, the one my granddaddy had me believing for many years were our kin; then we went into Arkansas and Oklahoma.

I'd never driven across the country before. It was incredible. It made me understand, like I'd never quite understood before, that there was so much to see, there were so many roads ahead of me, so many things that I was yet to discover. It made me understand, too, that even though Chris and I were in the same car, when it came to our lives, we were going in different directions, traveling at different speeds to very different places.

"You know what your grandmother said to me?" I was scared to ask. With Grandmamma Pressly, it could have been anything. I waited for Chris to tell me.

"She said that I should marry you." I snickered.

"Why are you laughing?" he asked, as if that was really a serious possibility. I glanced into the rearview mirror and saw where we'd been, and then I looked through the windshield to what was ahead of us. All the reasons were stacking up, one by one, in my mind. I thought of Miss Mills and the stories that I wanted to write and give to her. I thought of Miss Culpepper and how shocked she'd be to see me now, excelling in the one area she never thought I'd be able to master. Then I thought of my dad and our Thursday nights together, him twirling my baton and marching through the house. I could hear myself cheering with him, "B-e-c-a-u-s-e. B-e-c-a-u-s-e." I looked over at Chris, shrugged, and answered his question. "Because," I said. "Because."

tribe

Slowly, a circle was forming, coming into focus. A circle of people to whom I felt I belonged, but not by blood or location or any of the other everyday markers. It was something deeper, something magnetic, something that defies explanation. It was as if we were meant to find each other. And the instant we did, we recognized one another. We knew that we were members of the same tribe.

That's how it was with Ruthie Hathaway and me, except we were so young we just called it sisterhood. We didn't have any other word or way to describe what it was that made us feel like kin. The same thing was true of Lily Benson. Even before I left my mom's house and moved in with her and her folks, I knew

that there was a connection between us that was deeper than a
simple friendship. Just as I knew during the first few weeks I
was living under their roof that what existed between Mom and
Dave and me was a real bond, one that completely surpassed my
understanding. Mom and Dave weren't just Lily's parents or the
kind couple who had taken me in. They were my parents, too.

My relationship to Mom and Dave had no bearing on my relationship to my biological parents. One didn't trump or negate
the other. Mom and Dave weren't replacement parents or anything like that. They were an additional set, a bonus, the gift
that life had given me. And what a gift those two were.

When I moved back into Mom and Dave's, with the renewed
goal of becoming an actress, they went all out to give me whatever help I needed. I didn't have an agent yet, but like most
people who are just starting out in the business, I did have my
ear to the ground, so I was able to find out about auditions. I
got a little work here and there; I even got a small role in a film
in which John Ritter played my father. But those jobs were all
like baby steps, not terribly significant in the larger scheme of
things.

Even though I was still working a part-time job, I was perpetually broke. The business of being an actor is not inexpensive.
You have to get your pictures taken and have dozens of head-
shots and résumés printed. When you're auditioning for a role,
you're expected to come in character, meaning that if you don't
have the right clothes, you have to go buy them. And you have to
be able to get to your auditions. I had a car now, so I was mobile,

but the drive back and forth between Los Angeles and Orange County was burning a serious hole in my pocket. It seemed like every cent I got went straight into my gas tank.

Mom and Dave used to keep one of those plastic water-cooler bottles in their room. Lily did, too. Every night, when they came home, they used to dump all their spare change in their bottle. It was the working-person's automatic savings plan. Mom and Dave gave me a bottle for my room as well. I followed suit and dropped all my extra money into my bottle each time I went into my room. It was a good habit to develop, though I gotta confess that sometimes, when I was really broke, I'd only give up the pennies. I'd pick the silver coins out and put those back into my purse. Nobody ever said so, but it was generally understood that once the coins went in, they weren't supposed to come back out until the bottle was totally full and all that spare change actually amounted to something significant.

In a lot of ways Mom and Dave weren't so different from my biological parents. Whenever I had an audition, they'd stay up with me the night before and help me memorize my part. We'd each get a drink—a shot of scotch for Dave, some Grand Marnier for Mom, and a Corona for me. Then Mom and Dave would divvy up the other characters in the scene, and the three of us would toss lines. They always found a way to make it fun.

"Why do you always get to play the women?" Dave would ask Mom every now and then. Mom would give him this kinda snide look and she'd say, "Fine then, you play the women. I'll play the men." Dave would whip the script page up and hold it in front of his face. He'd clear his throat and deliver his first line in this hilariously high-pitched voice. Mom and I would look at him like he was out of his mind. "What?" he'd ask in his regular voice. "C'mon. Let's continue." Then we'd all just crack up.

It was just the sort of thing my dad would do. I could very easily picture my father with me, right there in that room, finding a way to make the whole process a breeze and making me laugh all the while. "All right now, Chicken," he might say. "You focus on your lines and I'll play everybody else." Knowing him and how good he was at imitating people in the stories he told, he'd probably travel from baritone to soprano to find a unique voice for each and every one of those characters in a scene.

Sometimes Mom and Dave would stay up until one or two o'clock in the morning with me, making sure I'd memorized each line and had my character down pat. When they were ready to turn in, Mom would get up and start heading toward their bedroom. Dave would lag behind, as though he was waiting his turn to hug me good night and wish me luck. The real reason he did that was so he could slip me his gas card or a nice, crisp twenty.

"Just so you can get there all right, kiddo," he'd whisper in my ear. "Go kick some ass tomorrow."

My mother was supportive as well, though in an entirely different way. She and Richard had gotten married. They'd moved from the apartment in Costa Mesa into a house in Laguna. My mother and I were talking more, becoming closer. And now that Richard and I shared the love of my sister, Becky, the two of us were finding ways to inch our way around the huge canyon that once separated us.

One day my mother called me to tell me that she'd just received a phone call from a producer who wanted to schedule me for an audition. It was more than a little strange, because I never gave out my mother's number, especially for work. Why would I? I didn't live with her, and given that it was a fairly new number, I barely even knew it by heart.

"She called the old number." Now that made more sense to me. A few years back, I'd done some work on a film but it was more of a modeling gig than an acting job. The producer probably still had my number from then. "And you know what's even stranger?" my mother asked. "It was the last day of the forwarding message. If she'd called tomorrow, she wouldn't have been able to get the new number. Now isn't that lucky?"

I phoned the producer back and got all the details. It was an audition for the lead role in a film. This was a really big deal. Unlike with my other auditions, I didn't have a script to study beforehand, so my reading would be cold, without benefit of any rehearsal or memorization. Also, instead of reading for a casting director, I'd be reading in front of the producer herself, something that usually came later in the process, if an actress was lucky enough to make it that far.

The next day, I drove into Los Angeles. I was excited, but I was also a big ole bag of nerves. When I arrived, Madeline, the producer, gave me the script. I didn't realize that a section of it had been marked off, the section that was to serve as the sides—the exact part I was supposed to be reading. I used the time she gave me, about forty to forty-five minutes, to read the entire script.

"So, did you read the sides?" Madeline asked. I had no idea what she was talking about.

"What sides? I read the whole thing."

"You what? You read the whole thing?"

"What did you want me to memorize?" I asked.

"Just come in here," she said. When I walked into the room, she handed me a few pages, the ones I was supposed to have spent that time learning. I went over the lines twice and then put the sides away. Thankfully, I have a memory that's pretty much photographic. I wanted this job and I knew that I stood a good chance. The very fact that I was even standing in front of Madeline told me that luck was already on my side.

"Oh, honey," Madeline said, "you can just hold the pages in your hands and read from them."

"That's all right," I told her. "I know the lines." So we began the audition. I delivered each line that was printed on those pages. I didn't skip a word, didn't miss a beat.

"Do you have an agent?" Madeline wanted to know. I shook my head. "A manager?" I shook my head again. She smiled. "There's someone I want you to meet." She gave me the number for a woman named Irina Tarasova, a manager. "Call her," Madeline said.

Irina and I were supposed to meet for lunch the next day at Jerry's Famous Deli in Los Angeles. I did not have a single cent to my name. Whatever Mom and Dave gave, I accepted graciously. What they didn't give, I didn't ask for. They would have readily and happily put themselves out to do whatever they could to make sure all of my needs were met—and that's precisely why I never asked.

I'd been riding on empty for days. I'd even taken the risk of running out of gas to go to that last-minute audition with Madeline. There was no way the car would make it into Los Angeles again unless I filled up. I took my plastic cooler bottle, which was only about half-full, to the bank and had them turn all those pennies into enough singles to make that needle move from E to F. I got to the restaurant about ten or fifteen minutes early for our appointment, and I waited.

The menu at Jerry's Famous Deli has over six hundred items on it—and that is not an exaggeration. I was hungry, to the point where my stomach was speaking up for itself, releasing slow, angry growls, which I had no choice but to ignore. When the smells inside the restaurant became too much for my poor little tummy to take, I went outside to look out for Irina, who had supplied a rather general description of herself during our hurried telephone conversation the evening before.

After a few minutes of standing on the sidewalk, trying not to call attention to myself, I spotted a woman getting out of an SUV and I just knew that she had to be Irina. It was like one of those moments in a movie, when time travels in slow motion, a warm light washes over the person being observed, and operatic, almost angelic, voices start singing, "Aaahhhh." She was beautiful, but not in an old—or even new—Hollywood kind of way.

Everything she was wearing looked like it came right off a

rack of vintage couture from the house of Chloé. She looked sophisticated and she exuded an air of confidence. Her walk was sure and steady, and her smile was familiar and unpretentious. She was beautiful in a way that was hers and hers alone. It was undeniable, yet it didn't mirror anybody else's idea of the word. Irina Tarasova was not a carbon copy; she was an original, the real thing.

We introduced ourselves, then we went inside, were seated at a table and given menus. The waitress came over to take our drinks order. Irina wanted a cappuccino. I asked for a glass of water. Irina gave me a funny look, so I added, "With some lemon, please." I said it in a way that I imagined to be cool and casual, as though it was my usual. Meanwhile, another waitress walked by us with a heaping plate of Italian food, my favorite, which she placed in front of the person seated at the table directly behind me. The aroma roused my stomach into rebellion again. I didn't hear it growl, but I think Irina must have.

When our waitress came back with our drinks, she pulled her order pad out of her apron pocket and asked us if we had decided on our meals.

"She probably wants to order something," Irina said to the waitress. Even though I'd had a brief phone conversation with Irina, her Soviet accent still took me by surprise every time I heard it. It was thick and exotic and musical. The waitress turned to me with her pencil, poised to write.

"No, I've already eaten. Thank you." The waitress turned to Irina, who was still scanning the menu.

"Let me know whenever you're ready," she said, before leaving.

"You're hungry. Why don't you eat?" Irina wanted to know. I sucked in my stomach and clenched the muscles. It was my way of telling it, *Shut up. Don't you go embarrassing me in front of this chic manager-lady.* It obeyed, at least for a while. I held my position with Irina and insisted that I wasn't hungry, that I'd already had a bite before coming to our meeting. You know, I may have been poor but I was also really damned proud.

Irina didn't buy my act and she simply wouldn't accept my refusal.

"Jaime, you're hungry. I saw the way you looked at that food. You need to eat. You don't have money? It's okay, because I invited you to lunch. Be my guest, please."

"No, really," I insisted. "It's not about money. I've already—"

"Let me tell you something," Irina said, leaning in over the table. Her tone didn't change, nor did she raise her volume. She didn't have to. That voice of hers was so arresting it made you want to listen up. "Nobody should ever have too much pride to not eat, especially when they're hungry. Not you. Not at my table. Now, what do you like? Get it." Her words got me all choked up. I looked down at the menu. Ordinarily, I would have probably been defensive, moved my guard up even higher. I would have felt like I was being judged, but I didn't do any of that or feel any of that. In fact, what she said made me realize that nobody, least of all her, would think any less of me for letting her buy me lunch.

I looked down at the menu but I already knew what I wanted. When the waitress came back, I ordered a plate of penne pasta with creamy tomato sauce and garlic bread, the same dish that the other waitress had delivered earlier to the table behind me. To this day, that is the only thing I ever order when I go to Jerry's Famous Deli.

While we waited for the food, Irina talked to me about the scripts that were currently out and the films that were being cast. She talked about all the roles she imagined I'd be perfect for, and how she would go about managing my career. I listened in utter disbelief. My career? Film roles I'd be perfect for?

Sometimes opportunities come into our lives that seem too good to trust. We get scared that the minute we start believing, we'll have the rug pulled out from under us, we'll wake up to find that it'd all been a cruel joke the world had been playing on us. I couldn't bear for that to happen to me. Yet I also couldn't bring myself to doubt the possibility that this might be real. How could I turn away from this woman who seemed to be offering me my biggest, boldest dream on a silver platter?

Our waitress brought the food. It was all I could do to stop myself from picking the plate up and pouring the food straight down my throat. I was starving. Irina continued talking while I fed my face. I was eating so fast that she started laughing at me.

"Slow down, slow down," she said between chuckles. "There's no race. It's okay. We're going to be together for a while. You have plenty of time."

That night, Irina called and told me that she really wanted to represent me if I would let her. I was so excited I nearly peed my pants. I had to pinch myself to get the words out.

"Yes, I would love that. It'd be great." She asked me to meet her the following day in Beverly Hills. She wanted to introduce me to someone. I agreed and wrote down the address. After I hung up, I ran outside, got in my car, and turned on the engine. I wanted to make sure I had enough gas to get me there.

The building was on Rodeo Drive, just a short block away from the most exclusive stores in the world. I parked and went inside, where I met Irina in the lobby. We rode the elevator upstairs to a law firm. When we walked through the suite's doors and entered the reception area, I thought, *Holy shit, where have I landed?* It was beyond posh in there. There was a gigantic bouquet of fresh white tulips on the receptionist's desk.

Irina told the receptionist that we were there to see someone named Gideon Fischer. We were told to have a seat and wait. The doors to the reception area were glass. Whenever the elevator doors opened, I'd turn and stare into the hallway, sure that I would see somebody famous.

"Who's Gideon Fischer?" I finally asked Irina.

"I'm hoping he'll be your lawyer." He had a strong, biblical name. It made me think of Goliath, the giant. I pictured a tall, muscular hulk of a man. I'd never had a lawyer before. I wondered why I'd even need one.

We were escorted to Gideon's office. When we walked in, he wasn't at all the person I'd expected to see. He was sitting at his desk. As soon as he saw us, he stood up. He was about my height. The desk looked like it was bigger than him. He wasn't scrawny or anything like that, but he also wasn't Lou Ferrigno. Irina introduced us and we all sat down. Irina began by telling him that she was now working with me, and saying that she hoped he would work with me as well. The whole discussion was surreal.

Once it was agreed that he'd be working with us, Gideon and Irina got down to the business of making plans, stating their goals—our goals—out loud. They threw around some big names—Seagal, Schwarzenegger—and went on and on about how they imagined me being perfect for starring roles opposite these leading men. Me? How in the world were they going to make that happen? I didn't have a résumé to speak of. It was all very overwhelming. There were moments when I felt as if I had fallen down the rabbit hole into a sort of Wonderland. Everything that had happened to me since my mother told me about the phone call from Madeline, the producer, required a serious suspension of disbelief.

It was while we were sitting in Gideon's office that I found out I'd been offered the lead in the film I auditioned for a couple of days before.

"Gideon will be negotiating the deal," Irina informed me. What deal? They offer, we accept, done deal, right? Apparently, not.

"We're going to see about getting them to commit to giving you a couple more films," Gideon explained. I said, "Oh, all right," because I didn't know what else to say. This was all new to me.

When Irina and I were in the elevator, on our way out, I told

her about how I'd been expecting Gideon to resemble something more along the lines of Goliath.

"He's more like a David though," I added. Irina saw the humor in my comment. She laughed with me for a while. When
the elevator doors opened, we walked outside. We'd parked not
too far from each other, so we crossed the street together. As we
were parting company, Irina looked at me and said, "But Jaime,
don't ever forget that David won."

First, a major audition with a producer drops right out of the
sky onto my lap. Then, within twenty-four hours, I get a manager. The next day, I get a lawyer. By day four, my manager tells
me that she's gotten me a business manager who will handle
all my finances. Now, mind you, I don't have any finances to
handle. Before the end of day four, my manager and my lawyer
have negotiated a three-picture deal for me with a studio. One
of those films, of course, is what I'd auditioned for at the beginning of the week.

That had to be both the longest and the shortest week of my
life. On the one hand, it felt like I had done a few years' worth of
living in those few days; on the other hand, it felt like I'd only
closed my eyes for a second. My head was spinning. Too much
had happened. I got sick. I had a fever, my muscles hurt, and I
couldn't keep anything down. My body was buckling under the
weight of too many good things. I was getting panic attacks. I
remember hyperventilating, having to breathe hard into a paper bag. I went home to Mom and Dave's, where I could rest. I
kicked my feet up on the couch and lay my head down on Mom's

lap. Dave turned the TV on, and Mom caressed my hair until I fell asleep.

It wasn't a deep sleep. Mom and Dave were whispering so that they wouldn't wake me, but I could still hear them. I kept my eyes closed and listened, just as I had that one time when I'd overheard them including me in their family plans. It was the day when I knew for certain that they had fully claimed me. I would be theirs, and they would be mine, forever.

"I don't know that she's really sick," Mom said. She was still playing with my hair. Her touch was calming. I didn't want her to stop.

"Yeah," Dave agreed with her. "I think she'll be okay tomorrow."

"I think it's everything that's happened in the last few days," Mom went on. "She just needed to take a break from it all. She wanted her mom and her dad." She was right about that, I thought. Mom was definitely right.

wait

If there's one thing that a career in the entertainment industry will teach you how to do well, it's wait. You've gotta wait to get auditions, you've gotta wait at the auditions, and you've gotta wait after the auditions to find out if you got the part. All the big breaks that had suddenly come flying my way—the manager, the lawyer, the three-picture deal—may have appeared to be carrying me in the direction of overnight success, but I knew better.

My good fortune certainly accelerated a portion of the process. There's no denying that. What happened to me in the span of a single week could easily have taken several months or even several years to achieve. It moved me forward by leaps and bounds, but in no way did it take me the entire distance.

Relatively speaking, I was still at the very beginning, had barely knocked off the tip of a massive iceberg. No matter what it seemed like from the outside looking in, I knew the rest would take time. No matter how quickly I seemed to be moving toward "making it," I still had a whole lot more waiting to do, because that's just the way things worked.

Modeling had truly prepared me for the all-too-common situation of "hurry up and wait." My picture had been chosen out of the hundreds of thousands that were sent in to agencies and model searches by hopeful young girls like me. My mother, Aunt Careen, and I had been flown, all expenses paid, to California so that I could do a series of test shoots. The editor of *Teen* magazine saw the results of those shoots and was impressed. My mother and I were flown out again, all expenses paid, for me to do another series of shoots so that I could be considered for a possible cover model for the magazine. Of the three girls they were considering, I was the only one who'd never had any professional experience. Still, I got the job.

Everyone, myself included, thought my future success as a model was all but guaranteed—and with good reason. It looked as though I'd grabbed that shiny brass ring, straight out of the gate. I'd moved to California to secure this seemingly inevitable future. And what happened? I waited, and I waited, and I waited some more. And as the time passed me by, so, too, did the likelihood of ever having the sort of modeling career I'd dreamed of.

This go-round, I wasn't gonna be fooled. I wasn't about to count my chickens before they hatched. Yeah, I was gonna cross all my *t*s and dot all my *i*s to make sure I was ready to walk through any door that opened for me, but I was also gonna keep in mind that that might not happen for a good long while, if ever.

My first memorable experience with waiting came long before any of that other stuff. And by waiting I don't mean standing in line at the bank and the dry cleaners, or sitting around your house wondering when the cable guy is finally gonna show up. I mean really waiting, as long as it takes, for something that'll change your life. I probably shouldn't even call it my experience, because it didn't happen to me. I was only an onlooker, observing from a distance. Nevertheless, it made an impression on me.

I was about six years old, in the car with Grandmamma Pressly. As we were approaching an area not too far from Bynum, one of the public elementary schools in town, we saw a bunch of folks just kinda standing around. It wasn't a usual sight, so I wanted to know what was happening. Grandmamma Pressly told me that they were waiting in line for government cheese. It was early in the morning and that line of people stretched clear around the corner and almost down the street. Granted, I didn't know much about politics, but I gotta say, I was quite surprised to hear that in addition to everything else they did, the government actually sold cheese. Pleasantly surprised, because I loved cheese. My uncle Pruitt made the most mouthwatering pimento cheese in Kinston. Right off the bat, I got to wondering whether this government cheese was anywhere near as yummy as Uncle Pruitt's. I decided that it must have been, because if it wasn't, then why would so many people get up at the crack of dawn and wait in line to get some?

"Grandmamma, one day can we go and try some of that cheese?" She looked at me like I had just insulted her father *and* her firstborn.

"Jaime, have you gone and lost your mind?" she asked. "I'd rather take a dead dog, fry it up, and call it food." Well, that brought an abrupt end to my curiosity—about the cheese, but not about the people who were waiting there, and definitely not about how they could, literally, stand to wait that long. Judging from the length of the line, it would take hours to get to the front.

I never imagined those people could be waiting for any other reason than sheer desire, because they wanted to. I don't know why I'd never noticed them before, but after that first time, I saw them standing there every single month, like clockwork, just waiting. As I grew older, I got a better sense of what was really going on. Those people weren't there by choice; they were there because of a need I couldn't even begin to fathom. I felt bad knowing that they had to wait to get that need met. The whole thing had a huge impact on me; the image of those people standing in line stayed with me for years.

When you're a kid, time feels as slow-moving as molasses, probably because there's always plenty of it, more than enough to use and more than enough to waste. "We've got all the time in the world." That's what Granddaddy Pressly used to say whenever we went fishing. We'd be at the river house in Oriental, down at the end of the pier, right by the old sink that we'd hooked up. He called it his little slice of heaven. We'd sit, and then Granddaddy would ask, "You ready?" I'd nod and we'd count together, "One, two, three." Then we'd cast our rods and we'd start singing Otis Redding's "(Sittin' on) the Dock of the Bay" while we waited.

Granddaddy was a dapper man, except when he was fishing. Then you'd always find him wearing the same boots and belt and pair of pants. I think the pants used to be navy or some other shade of dark blue; they could have even been black, but they were so old, worn out, and messed up, they'd faded into a soft, dusty charcoal-gray. They smelled of fish, too. And those boots, they looked like he had used them to walk through the entire state of North Carolina, all over hell, and half of Georgia. Every now and again, when they started falling apart, Aunt Careen would take them in to be resoled. That would make Granddaddy so mad, because then they weren't as comfortable anymore. He'd complain that without the holes, he didn't have the breathing room he needed anymore.

Sometimes, when Granddaddy and I weren't singing away the time while we were waiting for the fish to come, we'd talk. A lot more times, we'd simply remain silent and enjoy the quiet of the day together. We could sit out there for hours and get nothing by way of reward except a deep tan and the thoughts we'd been tending. Or we could catch something and earn ourselves some bragging rights for the remainder of that particular stay at the river house. On a really amazing fishing day, Granddaddy would catch two fish at the same time, one on each hook. He was the only person I've ever known who could do that.

"Patience," Granddaddy would remind me whenever I got squirmy or sullen because it was taking too long to get a bite. "Patience. Good things come to those who wait." That would bring to mind those people I saw every month standing in line for their chunk of cheese. They'd be there in the morning when I was going to school, and a lot of them would still be there in the afternoon when I was going home. I would think about how I'd look out the car window and see some of the same people I'd seen earlier, and how they'd only be midway through the line even though all those hours had passed, hours I'd spent reading and spelling and writing and playing during recess. I was in complete awe of their perseverance, of that kind of patience. Whenever I thought about them, I'd feel so ashamed of myself for all the whining that I'd done and for losing faith so fast.

I loved it when we caught a fish. I loved scaling and cleaning it with Granddaddy right out there on the pier, in the old sink my family had hooked up. I loved watching while it was being cooked and, naturally, more than anything else, I loved eating it. What kind of person would I be if I didn't have the strength and courage to see myself through something that I'd had the privilege of choosing to do, to be able to wait for something that I claimed to want and love so much? I didn't want to know the answer, so I'd tighten my grip on my rod, I'd scooch closer to my granddaddy, and we'd start singing again.

―――――

After the whirlwind of a week that connected me with Irina and Gideon, my career settled into its own slow and steady pace, just as I had predicted. The three of us settled into a comfortable working relationship, and we committed ourselves to each other and to the long haul that we knew was ahead of us. I worked on each of the three films that Irina and Gideon had initially negotiated for me. They didn't end up being blockbusters, but each one was a victory for me and my team, a forward motion toward our goals.

There was this one time, early in our relationship, when Irina called me the day after an audition to tell me that I hadn't made the cut for the callbacks. I was disappointed, but it'd been my third audition that week, so I shrugged it off as part of the process. As it turns out, she was far more upset than I was, because the role was one she thought I'd be perfect for, a part that had the potential to take my career to the next level.

"Patience," I heard myself telling Irina. "Good things come to those who wait." Granddaddy would usually have to tell me that somewhere in the middle of the second hour we'd been sitting out there at the end of the pier. That's right about when all the excitement had worn off, when I'd flat-out forgotten that I was the one who'd jumped up and insisted, "I'm coming, too," when I saw him walking by wearing those stinky pants and raggedy boots.

I used to take those words of his to heart, turn them into a test of character. And as with any other test, practice made perfect. I taught myself how to hold out, how to hang in there. What didn't quite click for me until I found myself repeating those words to Irina was that in the midst of all that, I'd also learned how to stop focusing so much on the end result and appreciate the wait for what it was—an adventure, worth every minute of the ride.

face

Publicity in women is detestable. Anonymity runs in
their blood. The desire to be veiled still possesses them.
They are not even now as concerned about the health of
their fame as men are, and speaking generally, will pass
a tombstone or a signpost without feeling an irresistible
desire to cut their names on it.

Virginia Woolf

Guilin, China.
    The city is right on the western banks of the Li River
in the northeastern part of the country. It's a subtropi-
cal haven, one of the most uniquely beautiful places I've ever
been in my life. Guilin is definitely one of those "you've gotta

see it to believe it" places. There are two rivers and four lakes, and the entire city is surrounded by range after range of lush hills and misty mountains—Diecai Hill, Yaoshan Mountain, Lipu Mountain, Elephant Trunk Hill, and, beyond those, the Nan Mountains, which shield the famous Yangtze River.

The city is so picturesque it's almost unbelievable. It looks like something right out of a dream, or a movie. That's probably why it's been used as a location for so many films, like *The Incredibles,* one of the installments of *Star Wars,* and the one we were there to shoot—*DOA: Dead or Alive.*

Nearly ten years had passed since I'd signed on to work with Irina and Gideon. During that time, I'd worked consistently. I'd been featured in several films and television shows. I'd also been hired as a regular cast member on two sitcoms. What I loved the most about acting was that each job I was fortunate enough to get exposed me to new people and introduced me to new places, experiences, and knowledge. I had never been to China before, and I was excited about being able to spend so much time there, enough time to really get a feel for the culture and the lifestyle. My time in Japan had, without question, been pivotal, but I was so much younger, greener. Now that I was an adult, a more mature professional who had been out in the world a little longer, the journey abroad intersected with experiences, informed my perspective, and expanded my awareness in a way that was as fundamental as it was visceral.

We were scheduled to work in Guilin for seven weeks. Most of us were staying at the Hotel of Modern Art, or HOMA, which is about a twenty-minute drive from the center of town. HOMA is inside of Yuzi Paradise, a fifteen-hundred-acre estate. In the local vernacular, the word *yuzi* means "fool." A fool's paradise, this would be my home for nearly two months.

After we got to Guilin, we took a bus to Yuzi Paradise. At the entrance were these tall, ornate gates, which opened really slowly and ceremoniously. We were already blown away by everything we'd seen during the short drive. Things we'd never imagined we'd ever see in real life, like oxen and rice paddies full of workers wearing conical hats. What we saw once we drove into the compound really took our breath away. Every which way we turned, there were gigantic modern sculptures. There was a golf course, a greenhouse, and an atelier. The whole place was like a tribute to art and artists, right in the middle of nature at its most serene.

DOA: Dead or Alive was a martial-arts movie, featuring four female fighters. We'd been receiving martial-arts training for months before we'd even arrived in China. The plan was that we'd train for two more weeks in Guilin, and then we'd start shooting. Well, as it turns out, our little fool's paradise was square in the middle of a monsoon zone. We had to delay shooting for a couple of days, because the wind and rain started up right at the same time that we were supposed to.

Since we were all stuck inside, we decided to use our unexpected free time wisely and organize our laundry. Each of us was down to our last outfit and pair of undies, so we went through our suitcases, gathered up our dirty stuff, and sent it out to be cleaned. Later that same day, all the women had bags delivered to our doors. Inside the bags were the bras and underwear we'd sent out earlier to be cleaned, but they were still dirty. I didn't understand what was going on. Our translators explained to us that the reason they'd been returned was that in China, none of the domestic workers or laundry services would accept women's undergarments. They only washed the men's.

"So what are we supposed to do?" I asked. It wasn't like there was a coin-operated facility on the premises.

"You can either wash them in the river like the local women," we were told, "or, if you prefer, you can use the bathtub or the sink. But you have to wash them yourself."

"Oh no," I said, envisioning myself standing over a bathroom sink hand-washing weeks' worth of bras and underwear. After Guilin, we'd be shooting at other locations in China. There was no way I could do that for the entire four months we were supposed to be in the country. The other women were standing there, silent and dumbstruck, probably caught somewhere inside the same nightmare I'd just had, of having to shoot our scenes with dry prune-fingers. It'd have been one thing if they'd told us that they couldn't wash anybody's undergarments, and returned the men's undershirts, briefs, and boxers, too. So, during the day we were supposed to play these badass, butt-kicking women in the film and at night we were supposed to arm ourselves with some Woolite and a bucket? Oh, hell no. That was not what I'd signed on for. I pitched a fit.

"I don't really get why they won't wash women's underwear here," I told our translators, "but I also really don't care. They need to understand that we're working, and we're not from here. Take these bags back and tell them to wash our stuff. All of it."

Our translators ran through it all again, explaining at length that that's just how it was in China, but I would not accept no for an answer, so finally the bags were taken back to the cleaners. The next day all of us, the women and the men, got our clothes and undergarments back—and they were all clean.

It was only a small, and short-lived, victory. We had to go through the same thing again the following week and the week after that. Meanwhile, the men enjoyed the luxury of a full, no-hassles laundry service. Every week, they got their briefs and boxers back, spic-and-span. I couldn't believe we had to go through all that just because we were women. It got real old real fast. I ended up going to the producers and asking them to get us a washer and dryer. They did, and for the rest of our stay in China, while our male colleagues sent their clothes out to be cleaned, we women had to do our laundry—the intimate items, at least—ourselves.

At the end of our first week at Yuzi Paradise, a group of us ventured into the town with one of our translators. We'd been staying—night and day, work and play—inside one fantasy or another. We were ready for a taste of real life, Guilin-style, so we went to a marketplace. All of the vendors used makeshift wooden stands, like little kiosks. There were a few men, but nearly all of the stands were "manned" by women.

When we entered, we noticed that one of the vendors had added an overhang to her kiosk, a small slanted piece of wood, which, I guess, was to protect her merchandise from the rain. Hers was the only stand like that. The others were basic and, with the exception of size and inventory, identical. As we were passing through the general area of this woman's kiosk, a couple of policemen in full uniform walked over to her and said something. They spoke so loudly it caught our attention. All of us in our little group stopped and looked over at them. The tone of their statement was rough and authoritative.

"They told her that she has to take that wooden addition down right away," our translator voluntarily told us. The woman said something back to the policemen. Whatever it was, it sounded calm and polite. She even looked to be smiling. We turned and looked at our translator.

"She asked them why. She said it's not hurting anyone and that she put it there to block the sun and rain so her customers could stand under it and see what they were buying." We turned back when we heard the policemen shouting something at her. After that, they started ripping the overhang off her kiosk. The woman was crying as she watched them destroy her property. I didn't know what was going on, but it didn't seem right.

"Why are they doing that?" I asked our translator.

"Because they can," she said under her breath. After they'd removed the piece of wood, they threw it down on the ground and started stomping on it. The woman cried harder.

"No, no, no," she cried. *"Wǒ méiyǒu zuòcuò shì."*

"She's telling them that she hasn't done anything wrong. It was a misunderstanding." There wasn't any movement in that part of the marketplace. Everybody was standing and staring at what was going on. I was amazed that none of the other vendors, particularly the men, were coming to her defense. The woman reached into her stall and grabbed a long metal candle snuffer off one of the shelves. She started waving it at the policemen. Her face and hands were so red it looked like her whole body was about to burst into flames.

"No! No! Tíngzhǐ! Tíngzhǐ!"

"She's telling them to stop," our translator said. The policemen continued to step on and kick the overhang they'd pulled down, which was now splintered and cracked in about a dozen different places. When the policemen noticed the woman waving the candle snuffer at them, they both pulled out their clubs and moved toward her. She took a few steps back.

"Búyào dǎrǎo wǒ. Búyào pèng wǒ!" the woman screamed.

"She said, 'Leave me alone. Don't touch me,'" our translator told us. Then she turned to face us. Her expression was dour, as if she was the one who'd done something wrong. She cleared her throat. "We should go now," she said matter-of-factly and proceeded to walk away, deeper into the marketplace. The rest of us stayed frozen. We watched the policemen raise their clubs and bring them down on the woman's legs. One hit her in the shin, the other on the knee. They raised their clubs again. The woman was wailing now.

"Please," our translator called out to us from a few feet away. "Let us continue." One by one, we tore ourselves away from the scene and followed our translator to another part of the marketplace, where the noise from all the tourists laughing and taking pictures and haggling over prices drowned out the sounds of the unspeakable violence that was taking place not too far away.

Shopping is the great American escape—from damn near anything. I'd been anxious to buy something as a reminder of my time in Guilin. After what I'd just witnessed, though, I wasn't so sure I wanted to be reminded of it anymore. Initially, I'd had my heart set on getting a piece of art. It's what I usually got whenever I traveled to a foreign country. In this instance, it had seemed especially appropriate, seeing as how we were staying in the Hotel of Modern Art, which was situated right in the middle of an art exhibition. But I didn't think I had it in me at that moment to shop, let alone appreciate the beauty of a work of art. Then I saw her.

She was in the first store area we entered, painted in the most vivid colors. I walked away from the group to have a closer look. The paint was thick and textured, almost as if the artist had thrown away the brushes and opted to use her fingers. She was the only thing in the painting. She looked like a geisha, dressed up like a doll with her jet-black hair swept into a tight, decorated bun. Everything about her was feminine and expressive, except her face, which was totally blank. The artist had left that space empty; no lips, no nose, no eyes. She was a woman without a face. Not just a woman: the visual epitome of what a woman is supposed to be.

I bought the painting. It drew me in and, in its own way, helped move me past the trauma of what I'd witnessed earlier. Not that I forgot about it. I didn't. I couldn't. In fact, it might have been one of the reasons I was so mesmerized by that work of art. In my mind, the woman in the painting and the woman who'd been attacked at the marketplace were somehow linked. I couldn't explain it but I felt it, especially as the days passed and my memory of the woman at the marketplace's face slowly began to disappear, until it was as blank as the face of the woman in the painting.

It was a relief to leave China. After Guilin, we worked in Hanbei and then Shanghai. No matter where we were and no matter how different the food, scenery, and dialects were, there was one constant: the treatment of women as lesser creatures. I'm not overlooking the fact that as a foreigner, as an American woman, my interpretation of their culture might not be altogether fair or unbiased. I know that we Americans, regardless of gender, are used to a certain level of overall freedom that doesn't exist anywhere else in the world. But it was more than that. It was the way women were looked at and spoken to over there. It was obvious that at times we were merely being tolerated because we were foreign. We women, that is. The men in our cast and crew were looked at and spoken to with an unqualified respect. They were never simply tolerated; they were entertained, entitled, taken as is. And it just about drove me crazy.

When I got back home, I had the painting framed and hung it up on my wall. There were days when I would just sit and look at it, staring into the space where the woman's eyes would have been. It kinda reminded me of the *Mona Lisa*, even though the two paintings aren't even remotely alike in any way whatsoever. I think it was because the *Mona Lisa* was the only other work of art that had disturbed me in the same way. It was the closest I could come, by way of comparison, to the painting I'd bought in Guilin, because for whatever reason, da Vinci didn't paint her with any eyebrows or eyelashes.

Sometimes I would imagine a face for the woman in my painting. I'd sketch the features in with my mind. I'd give her a smile or a pout. I'd make the sun dance in her eyes or I'd make them cloudy and sad. But as hard as I tried, I couldn't settle on any one in particular, and that really bothered me to no end. I wanted her to be somebody specific, to send a specific message with her expression. Why had the artist painted this woman with no face?

"She sorta reminds me of my mother," a friend of mine said after seeing the painting, "and my grandmother." That friend wasn't even Chinese. She was a blond-haired white woman, like me. I looked at her sideways.

"Yeah? How so?"

"I dunno," she shrugged. "The facelessness." As ridiculous an answer as that was, standing there looking at the painting with my friend, I actually understood what she meant by it.

My mother is one of the strongest women I've ever met. It took me a while to see that. Truthfully, it took me a while to see *her*. I'd always judged her on my terms and with the values of my time, not hers. I'd easily been able to identify the strengths of the men in my family, but I guess I'd always taken the women at face value. And just like the woman in that painting, they'd come out blank.

A large part of my rush in wanting to get out of Kinston had to do with not wanting to end up like the women in that town, and the women in my life. It wasn't like there was anything bad or wrong with them. Their lives were good enough. But I wanted better than good enough, and, quiet as I tried to keep it, I wondered how they were able to find it acceptable. I was young and I failed to understand that for a majority of women the world over, what they had was about as good as it was ever gonna get, and they were trying with all their might to make the best of it.

Some of what I chose to believe were the most crystal-clear memories of my childhood featured my father rather prominently and all but rendered my mother invisible. When I would tell folks about the annual Christmas Eve party that my Grandmamma and Granddaddy Pressly used to have, I'd tell them all about how J. L. Pressly and his brothers would get loud and lively when they got to telling those jokes and tall tales of theirs. And that was a fact. But another fact was that at each and every one of those parties, their wives would be subjected to the presence of damn near every single ex-girlfriend or ex-wife that those Pressly men had ever had. Everybody knew that the Presslys threw a mean party, and even though they were exes, these women didn't want to miss out on the fun, so they'd show up.

How uncomfortable could that have been? All the Pressly women would get pissed, even Grandmamma. None of us kids ever knew that, though, because nobody ever said anything, not even Grandmamma Pressly, as feisty as she was. They'd just bite their tongues and suffer in silence, and let their men take center stage. See, I don't know if I could have done that. Knowing me, I'd have personally shown each and every one of those women the door. But that's not how women were supposed to behave. It wouldn't have been proper. Back then, especially in the South, a woman's strength was measured by how much—not how little—she was able to tolerate.

And my mother tolerated a whole lot, as did many other women. In the mid-1970s, when she got married to my father, women were barely able to get credit in their own names. I don't think I knew any married women in Kinston who used their maiden names; they automatically took their husband's name. Women were definitely in the midst of a movement, but when it comes to issues of equality and social justice, the South is sometimes slow about embracing change. To be fair, it's not just the South. Even today, there are pages and pages on the Internet, from blogs and from newspaper articles, full of talk about why and when Hillary Rodham Clinton is using her maiden name or not.

If I were to put myself in my mother's place, I'm not sure whether I'd have had the courage to do some of the things she did. Would I have been able to stay for years in a marriage that I knew for certain was over? Or give up my career and everything else in my life to move three thousand miles away because my teenage daughter wanted me to? Andrea Lynch grew up in a town no bigger than a minute. Finding a way out of the sort of anonymity that Grifton, North Carolina, had in store for her was not easy. She exercised tremendous discipline and took significant risks to end up in Kinston, running a successful dance studio and choreographing major shows there and elsewhere.

Yeah, I could definitely understand what my friend meant by facelessness. It made me start thinking about the painting in another way. Those Chinese policemen had harassed that woman at the marketplace because she wasn't conforming. Even after they'd torn down her overhang so that her stall looked like every other one there, she did something that none of the other women there dared to do: she spoke up. And she was punished for it.

The fighter in me was proud of her. I'd been ashamed of the other women there at the marketplace, the ones who hadn't said a word when their colleague was being beaten up. What I didn't consider then was that their silence may have been a form of strength. They were probably mothers working to feed their children, children who were waiting for them to come home that evening. A run-in with the police could have forever altered the lives of their families. I'd assumed that because I didn't hear their voices, they weren't taking a stand.

All of these thoughts led me to wonder if maybe the reason the artist had left the woman's face blank in the painting was that she'd wanted people to do what I had instinctively done, which was to impose my own image of a face onto that space. Maybe she'd wanted to send a message about how society viewed women, which was not at all. I mean, how long had it taken me to *see* my own mother for who she was, and continues to be?

joy

When Irina Tarasova talks, she leans in slightly; not as close as if she was telling you a secret, but close enough to get your undivided attention. Her voice has the same effect on me today that it did the first time I heard it. It's rich and raspy, like tiny pebbles rolling down a sheet of sandpaper. Even after thirty years in America, her Soviet accent is still thick. Her manner is very even and collected; she doesn't stutter, backpedal, or ever fly off the handle. And that lady's got a nose for success, knows how to sniff out the potential for a good deal better than anybody outside of a Vegas casino. I couldn't ask for a more ideal person to manage my career.

"Jaime," she said to me one day on the phone. "I have found the one, the perfect role for you. This, this is the one." I tried to picture her, on the other end, holding the script, probably all curled up, looking like one of those cardboard tubes at the center of a paper-towel roll. I liked what I'd heard in her voice. It started me wondering what the show was about, wondering what was written on those pages that made Irina so sure. Whatever it was, the twelve years we'd been together had taught me to trust her. So I just sat and stewed in my excitement while doing the one thing I had grown far too accustomed to doing in my career—waiting.

It didn't end up being too long of a wait, though. Less than an hour after Irina and I had hung up, a courier pulled into my driveway, rang the doorbell, and delivered a copy of the script to me. I almost gave myself a paper cut, I was in such a hurry to get that thing out of the envelope. I plopped myself down on the sofa and started reading. By the time I got to the double-digit pages, I had read more than enough to know how I felt about it. But I mustered up some self-control and got to the end before reaching over to hit that speed-dial button.

"I can play this part better than anybody," I blurted out when Irina answered. "I know this character. I know her backward and forward."

There are times when, as an actress, the role you're playing is of a person so utterly unfamiliar that you don't even know how to get into their head, let alone their heart. It's an incredible challenge. Then again, so is playing the role of a person who is extremely familiar to you, but in a different kind of way. I would dare to say that it can be even more of a challenge, because of everything you assume you already know. Human beings are complicated. They'll surprise you in a minute, turn left when you think they're going to turn right, flash you a smile when you think they're fixing to cuss you out. Knowing somebody well really only means you've gotten so close to them that the lines in their personality separating good from bad are too blurred for you to even try to judge them anymore. Some people also call that love.

This particular role was of Joy Hickey Turner, née Darville, one of the lead characters on *My Name Is Earl*, a brand-new television series that was being cast. Joy was a prickly, narcissistic, trailer-trash woman who gave everybody a whole lot of lip. She never stopped to think of what she was saying, just let it come tumbling out—unedited, often rude and insensitive, always politically incorrect. It was like she was missing a filter between her brain and her mouth. Yet there was something endearing about her brand of fearlessness, which had to be rooted in ignorance, the kind of ignorance that's said to bring about bliss. It's hard to blame somebody who is that oblivious of everyone else's feelings for all the bad things they say and do.

Interestingly enough, that was the exact reason why nobody ever held my Grandmamma Pressly accountable for all the horrible things she said and did. That, and the fact that they were blinded by their love for her. All except me. When I was a kid, I had no tolerance for her behavior, didn't find one lick of humor in it. Wreaking havoc on our lives seemed to be the sole purpose of her existence. She was a little piece of work herself, my grandmother, a real character. With the exception of money and status—which Grandmamma Pressly had a whole lot of—she and Joy Hickey Turner were one and the same. Joy's ex-husband even had the same name as my Granddaddy Pressly—Earl.

"I can do this," I told Irina. "You've gotta get me in for this."

"Already done," she said, in a matter-of-fact way. Of course it was, I thought. After all, this was Irina Tarasova I was dealing with.

Usually actors dress the part when they go in to audition for a role. They think it helps with the transformation from who they are into who the character is. Truthfully, that extra help is more for the benefit of the casting directors than the actors. It compensates for the imagination and general visualization skills that some of them might lack. This time, though, I made no effort to dress the part, so to speak. I had just come directly from another audition, and I was wearing blue jeans and a simple, fairly forgettable blouse. Also, I knew that Dava Waite, the woman who was casting that pilot episode, wasn't one who required all the bells and whistles and wigs in order to decide which actor was best suited for a role. Over the years, I'd been in to read for her several times, and she'd always struck me as being pretty much on her game, so I wasn't especially worried about her suffering from that type of myopia.

Most actors walk into the room as themselves. They greet the casting director and whoever else might be there, and then, when everybody's ready, they get into character and they act. I walked into that room as Joy, with a vengeance and an attitude, intent on claiming ownership of every molecule of air in there. There was not a single part of that character that resembled me, yet I didn't feel like I was acting. I felt like I had stepped completely inside of her, as if she was a head-to-toe costume that I could just zip up over me and get lost in. I wasn't playing Joy; I was being Joy. I could sense that Dava Waite knew this, that everybody in the room who was watching me knew it.

You know, there're times when you're trying out for something—I don't care whether it's cheerleading, the track team, a Broadway musical, or pole-dancing—that you just know you've outdone yourself and hit the nail directly on its head. It's one of those situations when, instead of being a nail-biting bag of nerves after the audition, you can walk confidently out of the room and say out loud, "Oh, snap." And that's pretty much what I did.

My callback audition was a week later. I went in to read for Greg Garcia, the creator of the show, and Jason Lee, the actor who would be playing Earl. I was supposed to read the lines from two scenes, but I only ended up having to do them from one. In that scene, Joy is hiding in her ex-husband Earl's motel room when he walks in with Catalina, who is a strictly platonic friend of his. Joy hits Earl upside the head with a phone, then she asks, "Who's the whore?" The question is crass and confrontational, not to mention disrespectful of a woman who Joy doesn't know and doesn't so much as stop to think of giving the benefit of doubt. Joy wasn't even supposed to be in the room; she'd broken in. Besides, she had no legitimate claims to Earl, not after having had an affair and giving birth to a black baby while she was married to him, a white man, and then tricking him into signing divorce papers when he was high on morphine in the hospital, recovering from an accident. It takes a whole lot of gall to remain shameless after all that.

I believe Greg Garcia envisioned and created the character of Joy as a force to be reckoned with. But each force has its own distinct level and intensity; they're all different. I delivered Joy back to Greg Garcia as a sheer force of nature, a hurricane, the sort of woman who can blow through your life and, on a whim, destroy everything in her path. I don't think either he or Jason Lee was expecting me, or any other actress coming in for the callback, to make Joy quite that raw. Afterward, they told me, "The minute you said that line—'Who's the whore?'—the part was yours. You didn't need to say anything else." Walking back to my car, I squinted at the sky, gave it a half-smile, half-snarl, and said, "Mm-hmmm." If Grandmamma Pressly was up there, and could see me, she'd know exactly what that meant. Touché.

Any ill emotion I felt for Grandmamma Pressly was fully reciprocated. I was her least favorite grandchild. Madison and Gayle were her obvious favorites. The three of us would have to go over to her and Granddaddy's whenever our parents went out. Upstairs on the second floor of their house was a really cool self-contained apartment, with its own kitchen, bathrooms, living room, and bedroom. Throughout the years, it had been used for various things. A few of Grandmamma's kids had lived there for short periods—before their marriages, after their marriages, in between their marriages, sometimes even during their marriages, but usually only in the beginning stages of the union. The space had also been a kind of salon, because Grandmamma used to do her clients' hair up there. We kids liked sleeping upstairs, because we could play house and pretend it was ours. It made us feel grown and there were no adults to interrupt that game of fantasy.

There was only room to sleep two up there, so Madison and Gayle would gang up on me to make sure I didn't stand a chance of being chosen. The most common thing they used to do—and I would fall for it every time—was lead me into a boisterous recital of one of those silly kids' rhymes. *Beans, beans, good for the heart, the more you eat them, the more you . . .* Madison and Gayle would fall into a sudden silence at that point and I, gullible little Jaime, so full of enthusiasm, would be the lone voice screaming out, *FART!* Next thing you know, Grandmamma would cut her eyes at me.

"Jaime," she'd call out. "My room!" Always, always, always, at the end of the day, I'd end up having to sleep with Grandmamma. Earl Pressly didn't sleep in the same room with his wife. His bedroom was clear on the other side of the house, and all you'd have to do to understand why was spend one night with Grandmamma. The woman snored like a bear. You'd have sworn one of those big black creatures from the Appalachian Trail had come and crawled up under the covers with you. Compared to me, and my little toothpick self, Grandmamma was about as big as a bear, too. And she was a leg-thrower, would lift and toss the whole thing—shin, knee, and thigh—horizontally across the bed. She'd roll over, and then, BAM, it'd land right on top of me, all four hundred pounds of leg. It's a wonder I'm still alive.

———

When I tell people that Joy reminds me of a bunch of folks from my hometown, but more than anybody else, she reminds me of my grandmother, they think I'm making it up. You can almost see them carefully turning over the image they have of me, and rethinking its implications. Some people have come right out and asked me, "Did your family live in a trailer park?" I have to laugh, because nothing could be further from the truth and because it's hard to imagine that in this day and age people still try to equate economic class with social comportment. Who you are is who you are. It doesn't matter how much money you've got in your bank account.

The similarities between Joy Hickey Turner and Grand-mamma Pressly are substantial. Joy operates a nail shop; my grandmother was the queen of cosmetology. Both of them are alarmingly attractive women, with their own sense of style. You couldn't have caught Grandmamma Pressly dead in any of the little racy clothes that Joy wears but she was flawless in her appearance, and her clothing was top of the line, and she was never without a matching purse and pair of shoes. Joy, like Grandmamma Pressly, surrounds herself with men, and she has to be the head woman in charge of those men's lives. And Grandmamma Pressly, like Joy, tried to be the boss of every-body, wherever she went. When she walked into a room, every-body had to notice. And if they didn't, they'd catch a huge, fiery piece of hell for it.

It's easy to love Joy, because she's trapped in a television, and, in that setting, she is larger than life. She's been given the per-mission to be—and we watch in total awe, wishing that we could also give ourselves permission to be—that gnarly, without any fear of reprisal. It's those core qualities and idiosyncrasies, undiluted and unedited, that we secretly envy. The woman's got a whole lot of heart.

"Whew. This thing's making me sweat like a whore in church," says Joy, in one episode, about her wedding dress. There was something Grandmamma Pressly used to say that was right along those lines: "Well, that went over about as well as a fart in church." Can't nobody tell me that the distance between those two women isn't short and direct—which is why I'd often find myself wondering why it wasn't as easy for me to love my grandmother, who was also larger than life and about as true as a nun's prayer to what was inside her heart.

Playing Joy on *My Name Is Earl* and having to get to know her beyond a superficial level in order to play the part well has helped me develop a lot of compassion for Grandmamma Pressly. It has shown me a tenderness and a vulnerability that I'd never let myself see before, but that was so much a part of her.

The soul of Joy Hickey Turner is a trailer park in Camden County. In the show, it's never made clear what state they're in, but there're only four Camden counties in America, and they're located in Georgia, Missouri, New Jersey, and North Carolina. If I was the betting kind, I'd put my money on North Carolina, but it's pretty obvious that I'm biased. Wherever that Camden County is, it's Joy's only frame of reference. She's never been anywhere else and she doesn't know anything else. She's brighter than she lets on and even though she acts like she thinks only of herself, her family is the most important thing in her life. It defines her and she draws her strength from it.

Kinston, North Carolina, for my grandmother, was like Camden County for Joy. She had so much history in that town, it was like she owned it and it owned her. She'd traveled around North Carolina and maybe a couple of other places, but she didn't really know any place like she knew Kinston. In a way, the world began and ended at Grandmamma Pressly's front door. She was definitely an intelligent woman, but she kept her blinders on, remained ignorant of new trends and developments or dismissed them entirely, because they were foreign to her and she didn't want to be bothered with anything she didn't already know. In her mind, her life was fine as it was; she was happy.

Family is what my grandmother knew best. She took great pride in being the matriarch. Her house was the meeting place for everything—reunions, holiday suppers, garden picnics, lazy Sunday afternoons. It was the glue that held us together as a single unit. She and Granddaddy made sure that underneath their roof and in between those walls and windows was a proper home. In order to accomplish that without too much quarreling, Granddaddy Pressly habitually deferred to Grandmamma. Her word was law. At least it looked that way from my vantage point. What I didn't realize was how reliant she was on Granddaddy, not until he passed away. His death just ate her up. I've never seen somebody miss another person the way she missed Granddaddy. It was his love that anchored her.

It would be years and years before Grandmamma Pressly eventually joined him on the other side, but when she did, she made her exit every bit as memorable and in-your-face poetic as her life had been. She died on Valentine's Day.

Irina and I were sitting at an outdoor café in the San Fernando Valley. It had been an unusually cold winter in Southern California, but the sun had shown mercy on us that day and decided to come out and shine. We had just finished one of our regular lunch get-togethers. We tried to schedule at least one every month so that we could touch base and have an in-person chat about both business and personal matters. The two of us were in an extremely jovial mood. The year was still new; we were barely out of the first month of 2007, but already it was promising to be phenomenal. A few months earlier, I had gotten engaged to a man who'd been my best friend for years, and I was pregnant, expecting our first child. *My Name Is Earl*, which was being praised by viewers and critics, had been picked up by the network for a third season. And I was going to be turning thirty. There were a lot of reasons to celebrate. Irina and I had just spent the better part of that afternoon talking and laughing about how far we'd both come since the first time we'd sat across from each other at Jerry's Famous Deli, to discuss my career.

The check had been paid, and we were waiting for our server to bring back the receipt. Irina leaned in a bit, as she is wont to do when making a point.

"Are you happy, Jaime?" she asked. It was a serious question, probably the most important of all the ones she'd asked me that day. To Irina, success without happiness was a meaningless achievement, a waste of time, money, and ambition. I was happier than I'd ever been, happier than I'd ever imagined I could be, and I wanted to express that to Irina, but "yes" didn't seem elastic enough to fit everything I felt in there. I placed a hand on my belly, breathed in, and tried to think of the words that would work.

Right then, somebody recognized me and walked up to our table. She was a middle-aged woman, slender and attractive, decked out in Ann Taylor, with the scent of a Thierry Mugler fragrance hanging overhead like a halo. Immediately, I shifted gears and prepared myself to respond to the greeting I thought she was about to issue. That lady opened her mouth and out squawked a near-perfect imitation of Joy Hickey Turner: "I don't care if she's Vietnamese, Chinese, or Chuck E. Cheese. She can't be learning English. It's cutting into my premium nail-decorating business."

I cracked up so hard I'm surprised my water didn't break. That quote was from an old episode, which aired in the early part of our first season. Earl had been teaching ESL to a group of immigrants. Some of them, with their newfound fluency, were luring away Joy's customers, and she was demanding that Earl put an immediate stop to their education.

It was amazing to me how the woman remembered those lines verbatim. But it wasn't only her. Those kinds of things happened all the time. People would walk up to me in shopping malls and go, "Oh, snap!" or stand next to me on the escalator and say, "Every time I walk out of my front door I win a beauty contest." They seemed to get so much pleasure out of pretending to be Joy. And they loved hearing those crazy things she says, most of which are thoroughly reprehensible, coming out of their own mouths. It was just the darnedest thing to observe.

Those interactions with Joy Hickey Turner fans always surfaced the memory of my Grandmamma Pressly and made me think of some of the whacked-out stuff she used to say.

"Let me tell you something, honey," she'd started in on me once, when I was at her house. I was in my teens, was living in California on my own, and had gone to Kinston for a brief visit. I begrudgingly sat down on the sofa to listen. "Men are like parkin' spaces. All the good ones are taken an' the ones left are handicapped. So go ahead an' pick one an' settle down."

Who but Grandmamma Pressly would say that to a teenager? From the moment I hit puberty, it seemed like she was trying to prepare me for the sort of future that contained a solitaire ring, a well-stocked kitchen, and a baby carriage.

Recently, I had been thinking a lot about my grandmother. The anniversary of her death was right around the corner. I had been thinking about how miserable she'd made me when I was younger. She didn't even have to try. All she had to do was be herself, and that would do it. And now, look! Isn't life chock-full of the most unpredictable events? Nearly every day I meet strangers who attempt to be her, to emulate her spirit. I find myself laughing, quite genuinely, when these people repeat the kind of caustic comments that would have made me cringe had they come from Grandmamma Pressly. How miraculous that the very personality I raged against is now giving me the one thing that Grandmamma Pressly was never able to while she was alive: Joy!

Maybe one word *is* expansive enough to convey an entire story.

"Yes," I said to Irina, shifting my gaze toward the cloudless sky. "Yes, I am very happy."

men, redux

There's nothing quite like a good love story. You know it's a classic when, in the retelling, you start spouting clichés like "it was fate," "there was a spark between them," "she got butterflies in her stomach," "it was a moonlit night," and "they lived happily ever after." Those are the sort of tales about boy-meets-girl that make you grab a box of Kleenex and cry so hard your nose gets stopped up with snot.

I put a lot of hard work and effort into creating the life I wanted. Of course, luck plays a part, too. If you could say that I was extremely lucky when it came to work, then you could also say that I was extremely unlucky when it came to love, the type of love that I'd dreamed of. If you put me in a room full of single men and asked me to choose one, I'd more than likely walk in and find myself attracted to the most flawed one of the bunch. He'd be handsome alright, but when all was said and done, he'd also probably be as useless as a pogo stick in quicksand. Sure, nobody's perfect, but there's a world of distance between less-than-perfect and the fixer-uppers I kept getting myself involved with.

After I got serious about straightening my life out and focusing on becoming an actress, I found that I just didn't have as much in common anymore with my old high school boyfriend, Chris Zucker. We went our separate ways. Like most young women, I did my fair share of dating. I went to lunch, dinner, the movies, the beach, and nightclubs with men who, I'd discover, were socially awkward, physically impaired, emotionally unavailable, too short, too tall, too fat, too thin, cheap, horny, nasty, mean, self-involved, addicted, obsessed, talkative, boring. You name it.

As the years passed, I watched a few of my friends meet their Mr. Right and get married. I'd listen as they told me every last detail of their story—how they met, who was wearing what, when they shared their first kiss, when they first knew he was "the one." How I enjoyed hearing those stories. They made me all the more anxious to find out how mine would unfold. I wanted a beautiful love story, one that I could tell my children, one that they would want to remember and repeat.

I'd read novels and watch films; I'd talk with relatives and friends. I'd pick and choose all of the parts of each love story that I, ideally, wanted to have in mine. For instance, I wanted a love story that was full of surprises, like when the woman dis-

covers after all these years of searching that all along the man
had been right there.

I wanted a love story that was full of common interests and
long conversations, something that would lead to a lifelong
commitment, to sharing a home together and raising children.
My version of what perfect love was and how it should play out
grew and changed with me, from year to year. If you'd have asked
me during my late teens or mid-twenties, or even in my late
twenties, to tell you what I thought was an ideal love story, you'd
have gotten three entirely different constructions. I'd be lying
if I told you that I could still remember any of them. But if you
were to ask me that today, the story I'd tell you about would be
the one that begins with Daniela and Almandeto, whose happiness and eventual hardship would, many many years later, in
its own winding and fateful way, impact my future happiness.

They were both born and raised in the Cuba that existed
before the dictatorship of Fidel Castro. She was a striking
young lady, with dark hair and dark eyes. He was a tall, broad-
shouldered, handsome man with skin like butterscotch. They
were high-school sweethearts, full of all the excitement and hope
that comes with young love. Even as the light of their country's
future was slowly being dimmed, Daniela and Amandeto held
on to their vision of a future together that was bright. They were
barely adults when they got married and had a son, Esteban.

Times were growing harder in Cuba. While other citizens
remained hopeful that the political tide would turn, Daniela's
family made a plan to leave their homeland. They knew it was

more likely that things would get worse before they got better. Damason, her brother, went and settled in the United States. As soon as he was able, Damason filed the paperwork to have the rest of his immediate family join him there. This was just before the mass exodus that brought wave upon wave of exiles to the shores of America on homemade boats, so it didn't take long for the government to approve their entrance.

When the time came for Daniela and her family to leave, it was difficult for her to say good-bye to Amandeto, but she knew their separation was only temporary. He had filed his paperwork, too. Soon, they'd be together—Daniela, Amandeto, and their baby boy, who hadn't even started to crawl yet. A new family in a new country. They thought it would only be a matter of weeks, two or three at the most. Never did it cross either of their minds, as Daniela was walking away with Esteban in her arms, that this would be the last time they'd see each other. But it was.

After arriving in America, Daniela moved from Miami to New York to California with her family. She waited and waited for Amandeto until it was clear that he wouldn't be coming. The two of them would never be together again, not in the way they'd planned. Eventually, she let go and tried to move on with her life. She fell in love again, with a man named Rogny. He was a free-spirited adventurer who found it hard to stand still in any one place or reality. They got married and had a baby, a boy named Eric. But the relationship didn't last. In less than a year after their son's birth, they went their separate ways.

Daniela was left on her own with two young boys to raise. Thankfully, she had her mother, who lived nearby. The family had settled in Hawthorne, California, in Los Angeles County. Daniela worked hard to make sure Esteban and Eric didn't want for anything. She had a full-time job working at a factory, but she'd sometimes take on extra work, whatever odd jobs that would bring in extra money. After her youngest, Eric, was in elementary school, the family moved to Orange County. They lived in Westminster. It wasn't one of the wealthier communities that the area is famous for, but it was a step up. The neighborhood they lived in was riddled with gangs. From time to time, they'd hear gunfire at night when they were in their beds. She'd call out to Esteban and Eric, "Get down! Get down!" She'd crawl from her bedroom to theirs and hold them in a huddle until the danger had passed.

Daniela maintained a close relationship with her boys. She didn't want them getting into trouble, so she made sure to keep a close eye on them. Both Eric and Esteban did well in school. Eric played sports, football and baseball. Since gangs were a way of life, Eric and Esteban grew up knowing a lot of gang members. They spoke in school and hung out on the courts, but when it came time for those other boys to go and tag or steal or fight or do whatever else they did, Eric and Esteban went home.

But the temptation of that lifestyle was strong and ever-present. There were times, during high school, when Eric would hop into his little Tercel with one of his friends and drive to Costa Mesa High to just kick it with some of the folks they knew there. If he saw some of the fellas he knew in the parking lot, he'd drive in, park his car, get out, and say hello. Most of them were *cholo*s, affiliated with one gang or another. Usually, they'd be out there chilling with their ladies, the *chola*s. A few times, he even saw them with a white girl. She'd be standing there, talking or laughing with them, a bunch of Bloods, in her blue jeans and blue Yankees baseball cap.

"Oh, she's that model chick," his friend told him when he'd asked about her. He looked over at the girl and caught the *chola*s giving her the evil eye. He shook his head and thought, *Crazy. That situation's got trouble written all over it.*

"Yo, Eric, you gonna roll with us tonight?" his friend asked. A part of him wanted to, but he knew that when you were with those guys, anything could happen. That's what made it so appealing. But what always followed the idea of that kind of fun was the idea of his mother finding out he'd been involved with a gang. It'd just break her heart and make her mad, to the point where she'd probably break his limbs.

"Nah," he said. "I'm gonna go home."

Music was the one temptation that Eric didn't deny himself. He couldn't get enough of it. When he was home, he'd listen to the radio, play records and CDs. He'd watched a guy he knew from the neighborhood, a DJ, spin records once, and in that instant he knew that he'd stumbled on something real, something he wanted to do. He was only sixteen, at that age when kids start trying to figure out what they want to do when they get out into the "real" world. It wasn't like a career—any career—in music was a practical option for him. He wasn't thinking that far ahead. He was only thinking of what made him happy.

One day, when he was driving down the freeway on his way home after dropping his friends off, a huge Ford 150 truck slammed into his Tercel. The impact was so hard it knocked his pull-out radio right out of its compartment, in the middle of a song he liked. Considering that his car was completely totaled, Eric wasn't hurt that badly. He did have to attend physical therapy and give up sports for a while. That old Tercel wasn't worth much, and he'd racked up a slew of medical bills, but when everything was accounted for, Eric received a settlement check for three thousand dollars.

It was a lot of money for a working-class family, but Daniela respected the fact that it was Eric's money. It was compensation for his suffering, his inconvenience, his loss; so when Eric asked her if he could use a portion of that money to buy a DJ system, she said, "Yes, on one condition." He wasn't allowed to take it out of the house. Daniela was well aware kids were killing each other over things as trivial as tennis shoes. She wanted to encourage Eric to pursue his passion for music, but she didn't want it to cost him his life.

He bought the system and used it at home. The older brother of Frank, one of his buddies, had been a DJ and he'd quit to follow another interest. Frank gave Eric two crates of records that had belonged to his brother. Eric used those to practice. He'd spin records at home and rehearse his intros and jokes in front of Esteban and his mother.

After a couple of years, Eric started DJ-ing house parties for friends. He was good and word got around. Before long, he was getting gigs all over Orange County. He also had a regular gig at a nightclub. He'd get so much work that he'd double-book himself and have to get another DJ to fill in for him at a gig.

Vivica James, a Costa Mesa High girl who he'd been acquainted with for years, called and asked if he'd DJ a party for a friend of hers, some actress who'd also gone to Costa Mesa High. He agreed, they settled on a rate, and confirmed the date. A couple days before the gig, he realized that it was on the same night he was scheduled to DJ at the nightclub. It was a special night, too. A bunch of his old buddies were supposed to be coming to the club. Eric found a way to take care of it so that everybody would be happy. He called a friend of his and asked him to take care of the actress's birthday party. His friend was available and said he'd take the gig, so it all worked out.

The following year, Eric threw a huge birthday party for himself. It was a packed house and the music was incredible. Most of the people there were his friends but there were also friends of friends and total strangers, people who'd come because they'd heard about it and recognized his name from all the DJ-ing he'd been doing over the last few years.

The party had been going strong for a couple of hours when a girl walked up to him and said, "You're Eric, right?" She had on jeans and was wearing her Kangol hat all low, but not too low.

"Yeah, I'm Eric."

"You owe me," she said. It wasn't a joke. She was dead serious. He looked at her again. Her face was familiar but he couldn't place it.

"Owe you what?" he asked.

"I paid for you to come DJ my birthday party. You didn't come. You sent somebody else instead. You owe me."

If you haven't figured it out by now, that girl was me. And that night was the beginning of what would blossom into a good, solid friendship. There was a connection between us, a spark. But I took it as a spark of recognition, not of romance. He was my kind of people, yet another member of my tribe.

After that initial meeting, our lives kept intersecting, sometimes by accident and sometimes on purpose. I hired him to DJ a few events I was hosting. I ran into him at various clubs when he was DJ-ing and when he was just out partying. Looking back at our lives, I can't help but wonder how often they'd intersected before then. We knew people in common. We'd both attended Orange Coast College at around the same time. We'd driven time and time again down the same freeways, the same streets, and hung out at the same places.

We had one common interest, music, and whenever we ran into each other, we'd go on and on about songs we loved. We'd argue over which bands we thought were better and hotter. From there, we discovered other interests and we learned to respect each other's opinions and personalities.

While I was aggressively pursuing my acting career, Eric was gaining popularity as a DJ and climbing the ranks. When it came to his profession, Eric had no shortage of talent or luck. With tenacity and through a series of chance opportunities, he went from DJ-ing and working odd jobs at a radio station to being the DJ of a nighttime show, which he took to the number one spot in the ratings.

As friends, we saw each other through the successes of our careers and the failures of our relationships. The time we spent together was always too short. We always had more to say, more to share. It was definitely one of those kinds of friendships that left you feeling warm and welcome. We spent a lot of time, years and years, getting to know each other. My assertiveness and ambition didn't faze him. In fact, I think it was part of what he liked about me. And I found his openness and vulnerability refreshing.

There's a lot about Eric that reminds me of the men in my family. His mother, Daniela, loved him and his brother in the same kinda way that Grandmamma Pressly loved her sons. And because of that, he was able to love himself. Thankfully, by the time Eric came into my life, I'd also made enough peace with my past to be in that same place of self-love. I think that's the big secret of surrounding your life with goodness, of finding a *good* man or a *good* woman. You've gotta love yourself. It's not an automatic guarantee for happily-ever-after, but it's sure as hell a promising beginning.

Falling in love the way Eric and I did, inch by inch and step by step, over the course of nearly ten years, has taught us to appreciate and accept each other as family, as people who would always be a part of each other's lives. With that understanding, we decided to do the most radical thing two people can do together: create a new life. Now that's my idea of a love story.

truth

Whoever came up with the brilliant idea that women should work throughout their pregnancies wasn't a feminist, they were a fascist. But it's become such a common and expected part of our culture there's really no way to get around it now, not without a doctor's note. I mean, imagine walking up and telling your boss that you wanna take the next eight or nine months off so that you can fully and freely tend to the morning sickness, swelling, cravings, gas, frequent urination, hemorrhoids, and hormonal upsets that come with your condition. Besides, who could actually afford to do that? Unless you're Warren Buffet or Oprah Winfrey, taking that much time off work comes with its own set of unpleasant conditions, like unemployment and guaranteed poverty.

What a lot of people don't realize is that when you strip away the celebrity part, working on a television series is pretty much like having a normal day job. I know it might not be exactly the same as being a secretary or a bank teller or a data-entry clerk, but there are similarities, like the fact that you do have to haul your ass out of bed every morning at the crack of dawn to get to work, whether you feel like it or not. And when you're working on a television show, sometimes your workday can last as long as sixteen hours. It was exhausting to maintain that kind of schedule while I was pregnant. I'd be so spent by the time I got home, all I wanted to do was fall out on the bed.

Never in my life have I slept as deeply or dreamed as richly as I did when I was pregnant. As soon as my head would hit the pillow, I'd cross over into this other world. I dreamed a lot about people from my past, except they weren't always in the past. Time would crisscross. They'd be with me in the present, sometimes as their past selves, sometimes not. Like in the dream I had about Ruthie Hathaway being with me as I was about to give birth. You know how they say people disappear into thin air? Well, she appeared right out of thin air as they were taking me into the delivery room, and she reached out for my hand.

"Don't worry, Jaime," she said. She knew exactly how nervous I was. We'd always been able to read each other's emotions. I held on to her hand and squeezed it hard. "You're gonna be just fine." And I truly believed her, too, because she knew what she was talking about. It was an experience she'd already had. Instead of stepping into her dad's shoes and taking over his businesses like everybody suspected she might, Ruthie fell in love, got married, and became a mother. I went to the wedding. I stood there marveling at the woman my best childhood friend had become, smiling at times whenever I'd remember how much mischief Ruthie and I used to get ourselves into. For a while there, we were everything to each other.

In the dream, I turned and told Ruthie how much I still loved her, but the person I saw, the person who was holding my hand wasn't the Ruthie who was now married with children, it was the thirteen-year-old tomboy Ruthie.

"I love you, too, Jaime," she said in her little-girl voice. "Maybe when you're done, you can ride your bike over to the house. Beau's driving me crazy with those bugs of his." *Huh? Ride my bike?* I hadn't ridden a bicycle in years, unless you count the stationary bikes at the gym.

That was weird. What's even weirder was when people I hadn't given a second's thought since the last time I'd laid eyes on them suddenly dropped into one of my dreams to have their say. The most disturbing one out of that category of dreams was the one I had about being in a boutique in Beverly Hills shopping for baby apparel. Well, I'm sweeping through every corner of the store trying to decide which items to put on my registry when who else should walk in but Clarissa Weatherford and her crew—Arlene Kinchelow, Constance Doggett, and Jessica Scroggins. They are the same exact girls I'd known, and detested, at Rochelle Middle School.

"Jaime Pressly," Clarissa says in that phony singsong voice she used to use. Except it sounds like she means it. "I do declare. Ain't you just a sight for sore eyes?" She starts walking toward me and the other girls follow. They haven't aged a day, and they have on the same color-coordinated preppy clothes and wear that same nasty poodle-perm hairstyle. Her kindness completely throws me off. I'm about to respond, say something nice in return, when all of a sudden Shelby Barksdale, Clarissa's boyfriend, comes into the boutique and stands right beside her. He nods hello to me and I do it back at him. He then gives Clarissa a knowing look.

"I wanna ask you a favor," she says. "Will you go out with my boyfriend?" I drop the box that I've been holding, which has a Sophie the Giraffe inside.

"Um, if you hadn't noticed," I tell Clarissa, "I'm about to have a baby."

I squat to pick up the box. When I stand up, Clarissa's posse has vanished, as have Clarissa and Shelby. They've been replaced by Stone Glazer and Skyla Martin—Tweedle Dumb and his gremlin.

"What does that have to do with anything?" Skyla asks. "It's only a date."

"Yeah," Stone adds. "I don't mind."

"C'mon." Skyla smiles. "Say you'll think about it." What can I say? I've gotten to the part where the dream starts to turn bad, so I will myself to wake up, and I do. Then I start my day.

It's funny how in dreams, the most unexpected people show up at the oddest times. Kinda makes you wonder whether it's all part of a sign, a hint about what the future holds or some sorta key to unlock the mysteries of your past. I believe the reason my dreams were getting increasingly more bizarre was that I was about to close one chapter of my life and open another. I was about to give birth to not one but two people, a new baby and a new me. I believe all those people who were showing up were there to help me through that transition—even people like Skyla Martin and Clarissa Weatherford.

The greatest emotional gifts, the ones that inspire the most growth, are often gained from our interactions with the people we like the least or have the hardest time getting along with. Thankfully, I didn't have too many people like that in my life or in my dreams. Even through all the difficulties we've had, my parents' love has been strong and ever-present—as has been the love of Junior, Aunt Careen, and the whole Pressly crew. Then there's the love of Mom and Dave and Lily, my adopted family. There's also the love of Irina and Gideon, and the rest of my tribe, which is now made up of a mess of friends. And most of all is the love of Eric, my life partner, the father of my child. Through everything, especially my pregnancy, Eric has been supportive and encouraging. He is a *good* man.

All in all, life has anchored me with *good* people; there has always been a lot of love all around me. I guess that, in and of itself, is a tremendous gift, one that I recognized even as I was being shuttled back and forth, into the past by my dreams and into the future by my waking life. Still, I sensed that the departure points and destinations of those nighttime journeys were not as far apart as one might imagine. And the more pregnant I became, the closer they became.

When I wasn't dreaming about people from my past, I was

hearing their voices. It started out with just Uncle Ezra, Grand-daddy, and Grandmamma Pressly, the ones who had passed away. Pretty soon, it was everybody. There'd be so much noise filling up my head, for a while I thought I was getting to be one sandwich short of a picnic. But talk about a trip down memory lane.

I'd be driving to work, watching the sun rise, and listening, just listening to those voices rattling around in my brain. One time I heard Aunt Careen talking about how she'd gone and had Granddaddy's boots bronzed, just like you would a baby's first pair of shoes. The very thought of eternally preserving those raggedy boots was enough to make me laugh all the way down the freeway until I got to the set. I wondered how Granddaddy would feel about his favorite weekend footwear being dipped in bronze and displayed on Aunt Careen's mantel like a prize or a plaque.

Those boots he wore when he was fishing weren't exactly representative of how Granddaddy Pressly dressed. He was a through-and-through Southern gentleman, full of chivalry and the love of God. He owned a dry-cleaning business, and, as such, was of the mind that if he could make clothes on a hanger look good enough to admire, then why wouldn't he do the same thing with the clothes that were hanging on his body? Under different circumstances, I might be inclined to say that Granddaddy played the part well, but I don't want to risk mak-ing it sound like he was acting or pretending to be something he wasn't.

Even retirement didn't change Granddaddy Pressly, except

in the obvious ways. He'd sold the business—to another Pressly, though, so that way it would remain in the family. Still, it was no longer his responsibility. Instead of working, one of the things he'd do during the day was go and play golf with about fifteen of his old buddies. The youngest one couldn't have been any less than seventy-seven years old. Even then, when there was nobody he had to impress, Granddaddy Pressly still got up every morning, pressed his clothes, and put on a tie. That's the kind of man he was. He put his heart into everything he did.

When he died, it seemed like everybody in Kinston came to Granddaddy's funeral to pay their respects. The place was packed, standing room only. The church had a theater-style balcony, which is where the choir was located. Toward the end of the service, the choir stood up to perform. Everybody turned and looked up at them. They'd left Granddaddy Pressly's spot empty, so it was hard not to notice his absence. The first song they sang was "Edelweiss," which was Granddaddy's favorite. On its surface, that song, which is a Rodgers and Hammerstein original from *The Sound of Music,* is about its namesake, edelweiss, a snow-white European mountain flower. But really, the song is about loss and the rediscovery of love. It's about rebirth. And when the choir sang it—with that big ole empty space in their midst and with us missing Granddaddy Pressly as much as we were—there wasn't a dry eye in that church. Everybody was bawling and boo-hooing. I didn't realize my granddaddy knew that many people, let alone had touched their lives. There was a piece of him, a piece of his memory, which belonged to every single person in that church.

I suppose the reason Aunt Careen had Granddaddy's boots bronzed was because they were representative of a more private part of him. They were representative of how we, his family, knew him. Those holey, ripped-up boots were but one of Granddaddy's requirements for relaxation and joy while he was at the river house. The others were those nasty, fish-stained pants; his fishing rod; every family member who was within driving distance of Oriental; and a radio blasting Steve Hardy's "Original Beach Party," a show he'd been listening to for years. At least that's how I remember it. But then again, memory can be discriminating.

Grandmamma never gave a hoot what anybody thought about her, but the Lord wasn't just anybody. The closer she got to leaving this life, the more she got to worrying about where she was gonna end up next. Grandmamma didn't want her soul being damned to fire and brimstone for all eternity, so she devised a rather crafty way to do right and get in good with the Lord before her judgment day.

I knew that Grandmamma was about to go soon. I could hear it in her voice whenever I talked to her. She was tired, ready to go to heaven to meet up with her husband, Earl, so they could finish the forever they'd vowed to each other. I wanted to see her one last time, to say my good-byes. I traveled to Kinston with the guy I was dating at that time. He was anxious to meet Grandmamma Pressly. He'd heard so much about her, she was like a legend to him. All he wanted was to see her in action, being the person he'd come to know through all the stories I'd told.

When we got to Grandmamma's hospital room, she welcomed

the both of us like the sweet li'l ole lady she never was. She patted a place beside her on the bed for me to sit down.

"Jaime," she said. "I just want you to know how proud I am
of you. You just went out there and did well for yourself. You did
the Pressly name proud. Now don't you ever forget how much I
love you." I was stunned, and so was my then-boyfriend, who
was expecting to hear something more along the lines of "It's
so damned quiet in this place you can hear a rat pissing on
cotton," or "Whew, I'm about as full as a tick," which is what
Grandmamma always said after a good meal. But that wasn't the
woman we met. That Mary Anna Pressly was a stranger to me and
everybody else who got a heaping dose of kindness from her.

Despite all her tacky comments and untoward behavior,
Mary Anna Pressly wanted to be remembered as a woman who
loved deeply and truly. She didn't want any of us to forget that
when all was said and done, her heart was a whole lot bigger
than her mouth. And she was a woman who always got her way.
That's why she sealed her deal with the Lord and died on Valentine's Day.

Her funeral was the complete opposite of Granddaddy's. She
had always been larger than life, so it was hard for us to believe
she was gone. It was almost like she was gonna walk in at any
minute and chastise us for talking about her behind her back.
Everybody had their Mary Anna Pressly experience to share.
It wasn't until she was about to be put into the ground that it
hit us: Grandmamma Pressly was really gone. The matriarch of
our family had died. That's when we began to cry.

By now, you're probably thinking I spent my entire pregnancy revisiting the significant episodes of my life and being haunted by the ghosts of Presslys past. That's not altogether too far from the truth.

But, you see, I was about to have a baby—and babies change everything. My brother Junior and I had both discovered that. My birth had challenged Junior to change his life, then my sister Becky's birth had challenged me to do the same. What challenges could there be left for my son, Dezi, to issue? I didn't know, and I didn't want to be caught by surprise, so I started going over every little detail with a fine-toothed comb. I wanted to take stock of my life, to be honest with myself about where I was and who I was.

I'd worked myself to the point of exhaustion, because that's what I knew: you find something you love, something you're good at, and you do it until you drop. It's what was handed down to me, the drive and the work ethic I'd been taught. Frankly, I didn't know what was gonna come next, after Dezi was born. I'd heard about mothers who'd given birth only to discover, to their surprise as much as anybody else's, that they no longer wanted to return to a job outside the home until their child was much older. I wanted to give myself that option, the ability to create a new future, one that I may not have ever imagined before.

And then, of course, there were the stories themselves. They were a vital part of that process of self-investigation. I've said before that the reason I was never able to tell my own stories when I was younger was that my experiences were still being shaped; I was yet to earn my scars, yet to survive any major storms. So instead of telling stories, I'd repeat them. I'd mimic a storytelling style that I admired, and I would repeat, verbatim, how I'd heard the story being told. I didn't even understand half of what I'd said, didn't know why the person I'd mimicked had chosen to pause in specific places or place emphasis on certain words. Those subtleties went right over my head. No wonder the kids who heard my stories would usually ask, "Was that really a true story?"

I'd always nod and say, "Ya damned straight it was," even if I wasn't one hundred percent positive. I'd always assumed that the truth was in the telling. I thought that the act of living—seeing and doing things—gave people license to stretch their truths whenever and however they saw fit, which is why people always claimed that truth was stranger than fiction.

Truth is all about perspective, the vision a person chooses to hold. It is personal and it fluctuates based on mood. There's never any logic to the sequence of events, and yet everything still manages to be resolved, to come full circle. That's what makes it so strange.

Collecting and telling those stories during my pregnancy made me see that I wasn't totally wrong in my assumptions. I learned something new about myself each time I told and re-told a story, even if it was the same story. The same goes for everyone else, too. The more stories I told about Aunt Careen, my mother and father, Mom and Dave, Ruthie Hathaway, or any of my uncles, the more real they became to me.

I guess that's one of the reasons my family was always so keen on sharing their stories with everybody. It was a way to get whoever was listening to hold on to a piece of their life, an attempt at immortality. The truth of who we are exists in our stories. That's why people write books and make films and television shows. That's why we keep scrapbooks and photo albums: so that we can share our stories. It's the way we make sure we are remembered to our grandchildren and great-grandchildren, the ones we'll never meet but who will carry our names as their own.

So now you understand why I needed to find my voice and learn how to tell these stories. I wanted to welcome this baby into the world with an army of ancestors by my side, and with me sharing the truth of who we are.

mama

Mother's Day, 2008
Dear Dezi,

 The second they put you in my arms, tears started pouring down my face. This warm, placid feeling washed over my entire being. You were only six pounds, three ounces, so tiny in comparison to me. I felt like some sort of Superwoman, knowing that I made you, that you were once this little creature moving around in my womb, elbowing and kicking me for the last several months. I was in complete awe of you, of how alert you were. Your beautiful eyes were wide open from the get-go—and the instant I looked into them, I saw that they were my eyes, my mother's eyes. I know most babies are born with blue eyes, but yours were a different kind of blue. They were my kind of blue, my mother's kind of blue, and even though I knew you weren't able to focus yet, you looked straight up at me as if you were. And I knew you could see, that you could look back through generations and see who you are, who you were meant to be, and why you chose us to give you that heritage. I knew the instant I looked into your eyes that your vision was my future. You were seeing me not as I used to be, but as I would be forever in your eyes. You took a deep breath and then let out a loud sigh of relief. So did I. The day had finally come. I finally got to meet the man of my dreams, the love of my life: you, my sweet, sweet Dezi James.

You arrived at 7:31 A.M. on May 11, 2007. You definitely took your time, because my water broke on a Wednesday, and I stayed in the hospital waiting for you for three days. They monitored you to make sure you weren't in any danger. And there you were, on the screen, a rock star. You were as stubborn as I am, insisting on coming out when you were good and ready, not when everybody else wanted you to.

Your father and I brought you home on May 13, Mother's Day. It was the most amazing gift you could have ever given me. All I've ever wanted in life was to be a great mom. All I've ever learned, everything I've ever fought or worked for, it was in preparation for this moment. As a small child, every night I would rock each one of my dolls to sleep before I went to bed. It would drive my parents crazy, because I was always late, up way past my bedtime, because of it. It was amazing to know that the day I'd been waiting for my whole life had come at last, the day when I was finally given the name "Mama." And that's who you saw when you looked at me, wasn't it? Your mother. The woman you'd call "Mama."

You will never fully understand the weight of importance you've brought to my life. For so long, I have worked and struggled and dreamed, and yes, I've done well for myself, but there was always a void. For years, I would buy houses and fix them up only to sell them as soon as they were nice enough to call home. I couldn't seem to find the right place for myself. I was always lonely. No matter how much money I had or how magnificent the house was, whenever I stepped foot inside, what greeted me was sadness.

Someone very famous once told me, as we were watching her two kids play, that once you have a child, you will never ever feel alone again.

"No matter where you go, Jaime," she said, "you will always have someone waiting for you when you get home, someone who loves you more than life and can't wait to see your face." That statement resonated in my head for years. I used to wonder when I would have a child of my own. I used to wonder what you would look like when you got here, what it would feel like to hold you in my arms. You, my son, were so wanted, so needed. I don't want you to ever doubt or forget that.

The moment I found out I was pregnant, I flipped. In the bathroom cabinet were three extra pregnancy tests, which I immediately used, one right after the other. Then, the following morning, I sent your dad out to the drugstore to buy five more. All of them, of course, came out positive. But I wanted to be sure. I needed to be sure. Having you meant that much to me.

Two and a half months after you were born, I turned thirty. I was excited to put my twenties behind me. I had, in every way possible, officially crossed the threshold into womanhood, into motherhood. There were bigger and better things to move on to. There was you, and there was your father—our little family.

I've always known that babies come into your life and lift you up, make you shine. I didn't know how you were going to do it, Dezi, but I knew you would. And you didn't waste any time staying true to that promise. Just two months after my thirtieth birthday, I won an Emmy in the category of Best Supporting Actress in a Comedy Series. It was for my portrayal of the character Joy in My Name Is Earl. *It was the second greatest thing that had ever happened in my life. Do I even need to tell you that the first greatest thing, without a doubt, was you?*

You know, I spent a long time trying to figure out what it was about the men in my family that made them such good people. And then, when I met your father, I realized what it was: each and every one of them had a close relationship with his mother. But realizing it and understanding it, I mean truly understanding it, were two different things. It is only now, because of you, that I really get it. I know now why that relationship was such a significant thing to them, why it brought out such goodness in them, because I understand, in a way I never could before you came along, the love between a mother and her son. It is a bond no one can or will ever break.

Dezi, this book of stories is for you. It's a present from me to you, an explanation of the things that happened, the people I knew and loved before you. I want you to know all of this, to know all of them. I want you to know me, the girl I was before you, so you can appreciate the woman I've become because of you.

One of my favorite quotes is by Socrates. He said, "True knowledge exists in knowing that you know nothing. And in knowing that you know nothing, that makes you the smartest of all." There are so many things that I wish for you, so many achievements that I wish for your life. You will, obviously, grow up to have your own dreams and hopes, some of which may be in line with the ones I have for you and others that will be yours alone, based on goals you've set for yourself. Whatever it is that you try to achieve in your life, I hope you always keep your mind and your soul open to new ideas and opinions. To be human is to be imperfect. Each of us is going to make mistakes. It's through those mistakes that we gain wisdom and get the opportunity to practice forgiveness. It's the only thing that allows us to grow and move forward—forgiving ourselves and forgiving each other. It's a powerful and liberating gesture. But you probably already know all this, because you were born an old soul. I saw it in your eyes that very first day I looked into them. I felt it in your touch.

It's been said that children raise their parents every bit as much as their parents raise them. I can't wait to discover the information and knowledge that you will introduce me to. Already my life has been divided into two; there is "before Dezi" and "after Dezi." Before your arrival, I started closing all of the old chapters in my life. With your birth came the creation of a new narrative, one that we've already started writing—you, your father, and me—together.

ACKNOWLEDGMENTS

I would like to express my gratitude to the following people:

Mom and Dad for always supporting and loving me even when they didn't understand me.

Sissy Weil for putting me on the path that led me to where I am today.

My siblings, who have never failed to inspire and support me—especially Jim, for giving me such big shoes to fill.

My Granddaddy Pressly for his patient heart, and my Grand-mamma Pressly for her spunk and charisma.

And all the other members of my crazy, amazing, talented, and loving family.

Rod and Shelly Blythe, for giving me a sense of belonging and a place to call home when I needed it most.

Dawn Hail and Katie Owsley for offering me the strength of sisterhood and for always standing by me.

Lena Roklin and Dave Feldman for their vision, faith, and perseverance.

Dan Rivero for his patience and support.

Megan Pope and Lauren Blalock for being on my team and for believing in and supporting my vision.

Greg Garcia for bringing Joy into my life.

Eric for his friendship, love, support, and for our little boy . . . Dezi James.

Meri Nana-Ama Danquah for helping me write a book that is true to who I am. For helping me get through this difficult process of reliving my past and understanding my present. Without you this book would have never been written. You are truly an inspiration to me and I thank you for all your hard work, time, and our amazing new-found friendship.

My agent, Jennifer Joel; my editor, Laurie Chittenden; and the folks at HarperCollins for believing in this project.

Many thanks to all my friends and colleagues whose names I could not mention because of space limitations. Please know that you all mean the world to me.